C000212980

The cartoonist Rupert Besley has l   has
long hoped someone else might p   let
fellow-newcomers and non-experts in on some of the island's best secrets. ...uch
of the last three years have been spent dragging fellow-researchers (wife and son)
round and round the Island coastline in a bid to do just that.

Rupert Besley is well-known for his postcards depicting the hazards of
holidaymaking under British skies, and his cartoons have appeared in various
publications, including *Private Eye, Punch* and *The Times Educational Supplement*. In
1992 a one-man exhibition of his work was held in Newport, featured locally on
television. His published works include two cartoon collections, a children's joke
book and a spoof guide to Scotland, still a bestseller north of the border. Locally
he is best known for his regular slot in *The County Press*.

THE ISLE OF WIGHT BEACH GUIDE

RUPERT BESLEY

THE DOVECOTE PRESS

First published in 1993 by the Dovecote Press Ltd
Stanbridge, Wimborne, Dorset BH21 4JD

Photoset in Sabon by the Typesetting Bureau
Wimborne, Dorset
Printed and bound by Biddles Ltd, Guildford and King's Lynn

ISBN 1 874336 01 6

While every reasonable care has been taken in compiling this book, the author
and publisher regret they cannot take responsibility for any errors,
omissions or changes in the details given.

CONTENTS

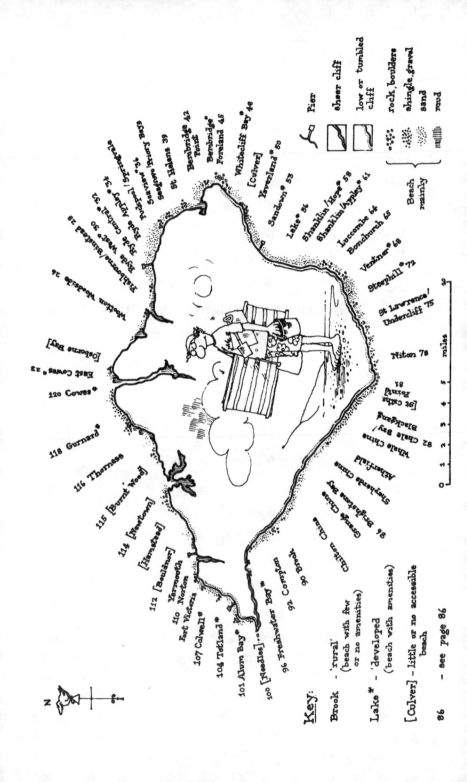

INTRODUCTION

The Isle of Wight may not have the clearest waters, emptiest beaches or softest sands, but it does cram into a small space with a pleasant climate as great a variety of coastal scenery as anywhere in Britain. The age-old tug-of-war between erosion and upheaval of the earth-crust has left the Island with a coastline full of interest: high chalk cliffs, long sandy bays, salt-marshes, estuaries, rocky coves and shingly beaches. Each is a favourite spot for someone.

A rough diamond in shape, the Isle of Wight has a coastline of between 57 and 65 miles, depending on the state of tide and amount of river estuary included in the calculations. The northern coast is mostly quiet woodland sloping down to a muddy shoreline, best enjoyed by wading birds and Solent sailors. The south-eastern coast belongs to the holidaymaker, and has the best sandy beaches and holiday attractions. The south-west coast, the 'Back o' the Wight', is, by comparison, wild and exposed, with crumbling cliffs dropping on to gravelly beaches tumbled by surf.

This last section (and around Newtown) enjoys special status as a Heritage Coast and Area of Outstanding Natural Beauty. About a quarter of the Island coastline is overlooked by development; the rest is rural and relatively wild. It is official policy to keep things this way. Efforts are being made to improve facilities in developed areas, towards Blue Flag standards where possible, whilst in the unspoilt sections car-parks, loos and like attractions are kept to a minimum.

There is no agreed definition of 'beach'. Forget the sun-spangled, palm-fringed sands of the brochures – this is Britain. A beach here is perhaps best defined as 'part of the shore where a small child can spend a happy hour with bucket and spade'. Nor is there a set number of beaches on the Island. A Royal Commission in the 1960s identified 52; officially, for EC regulation and water-testing, the Island now has 13 beaches. This guide attempts to provide up-to-date information on all parts of the Island coastline accessible to the public, insofar as is possible with something that is constantly changing. The Island's perimeter has been divided into 35 sections; some, like Brighstone, have several beaches lumped together. Elsewhere, as at Ryde and Sandown, the beach has been split into two or three sections. The main part of the guide is a Gazetteer of the Island seashore, clockwise from East Cowes, with notes and ratings for each section of coast under headings (Access, Beach, Bathing Etc) explained in the first part of the book. Reference material (tides, phone nos) follow the Gazetteer.

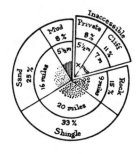

The Island Shoreline
(in rough terms)

The Island's main holiday beaches are all reasonably easy to get down to, but that leaves more than half the coastline along which access may be difficult, dangerous or even illegal.

Roads. Except from Yarmouth to Gurnard (and to some extent between E.Cowes and Ryde), the coastline is served by roads and bus-routes rarely more than half a mile from the sea. There are 480 miles of public road on the Island, most of them narrow, winding and hilly. They also fill up in summer. Each year 5,000 potholes are filled in – not dug, as some believe, and usually on the day you're rushing for the ferry. Island roads **are** different and should be treated with care and caution. This goes for parking too: leaving cars on verges close to a beach is not generally a good idea.

Parking. In peak summer weeks the Island population (124,577) is temporarily swamped by half as many again; more than a million car-trips are made over the Solent each year. Parking arrangements reflect these pressures. In winter seaside parking is easy – and free – in most places, including the fronts of the main resorts. From 1st April to 31st October charges come into operation, few of them ever at the same rate. Not all car-parks charge, Medina offering free parking at places like Appley and Puckpool. Elsewhere, even in summer, free space can be found by the water's edge for cars to stop and let those inside stare out to sea. Geography dictates that such spots are mostly along the low-lying northern coastline – Fort Victoria, Gurnard, East Cowes, Springvale.

To the Beach. All beaches by their nature require some climbing down to reach, Freshwater Bay from the car-park being the exception to prove the rule. Easiest to get down to are the developed sections of the north and south-eastern coasts, where steps and ramps from sea-walls and esplanades lead straight on to the sand. The south-western coast is different, having few points of access. Fifty years ago the Military Road opened up this coast to the public, but ways down to the beach are still precarious and difficult, especially in winter. Each spring new steps are carved, stairs installed and ropes dangled along the coast from Rocken End to Compton. Each year the wind and seas delight in smashing up hand-rails, dislocating steps and washing away footholds.

Private Property. Island beaches belong to a number of different bodies, public and private. Most welcome visitors. Those that don't (Osborne, parts of Binstead), make this plain on their notice-boards.

The average high-water mark is a critical line: above it, beach and cliffs are land which may or may not be privately owned, with or without public rights of way. Below this line is 'foreshore'. Almost all Britain's foreshore belongs to the Crown, is managed on its behalf by local councils and at low tide the public is usually free to walk over it. However, the Isle of Wight is different. When Isabella de Fortibus, the last private owner of the Island, sold Wight to the Crown on her deathbed in 1293, the sale did not include parcels of land (and foreshore) already sold off. To this day there are sections of private foreshore, between Wootton and Ryde for example, with jealously guarded rights of ownership and records to prove it.

Local authorities hold much of the foreshore and adjacent beach on Crown leases. South Wight Borough Council controls the greater part of the coastline, clockwise from Bembridge to Thorness. The remaining segment is Medina territory, though the two councils are due soon to merge into a single authority. But the councils' hold is far from complete; many parts of the coast are in other hands (Yarmouth Harbour Commissioners, Hamstead Estate, Thorness Holiday Park etc.), though still accessible along public rights of way. Some beaches are privately owned but organised for public use (Steephill, Totland, part of Colwell and Whitecliff Bay). Elsewhere, as at Orchard's Bay, private owners exercise their right to place certain conditions on prospective users of their beach. After the council, the main owner and manager of the seaside locally is the National Trust, which holds 15 miles of coastline, acquired mainly through Enterprise Neptune. Except for parts of Newtown Nature Reserve, NT land is open to the public, subject to certain protective regulations.

Along the shore. As well as being checked by private ownership at certain points, progress round the Island shoreline may be denied by cliffs, mud or tide. Victorian visitors were able to pick their way down a steep path to the sea at Scratchell's Bay; nowadays there is no access, except from the sea, round the whole Needles Headland — and lives have been lost trying to disprove this. Danger and inaccessibility continue below the chalk past Freshwater to Compton. At the other end of the Island, Culver is notorious, trapping holidaymakers each year at its base. Do not try to round it. At a number of points (marked as black spots on the map below) seams of hard rock run out to sea, creating ledges and cliffs where the tide comes right up. The golden rule is not to venture far round unknown headlands, except on a falling tide.

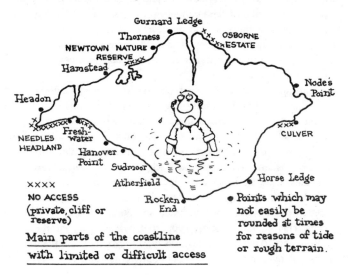

Gurnard Ledge
Thorness
OSBORNE ESTATE
NEWTOWN NATURE RESERVE
Hamstead
Node's Point
Headon
NEEDLES HEADLAND
Freshwater
CULVER
Hanover Point
Sudmoor
Atherfield
Horse Ledge
Rocken End

×××× NO ACCESS (private, cliff or reserve)

Main parts of the coastline with limited or difficult access

● Points which may not easily be rounded at times for reasons of tide or rough terrain.

It must be everyone's dream to discover a secret cove and be first to plant a footprint on the virgin sands. That doesn't really happen on the Isle of Wight, because the best sandy sections were the first to be developed by the holiday trade. The more lonely a beach, the more likely it is to be of mud or rock. But deserted beaches are to be found and not just in winter. Beachgoers are creatures of habit, frequenting the same spot at the same time of day. Walk on a bit or come back at a different hour and you may well find you have the beach to yourself. Divide the coastline of England and Wales by its population and it comes to about 4 inches per person; on the Isle of Wight it's more like 30 inches each, though less in summer.

Beach formation. All beaches are in a state of constant change, altered subtly by each tide and more noticeably with each season. Winter-storms sweep off loose material, while summer seas replace the sand on rocky platforms and exposed clays. Annual variations soon mount up – in the last century Ryde was muddy and Ventnor mostly sand. Stones and sand are always on the move – backwards, forwards and especially along. The sea acts as a sanding-block, smoothing off the coastline. That the job is never done and coast no neat straight line is due to the unequal hardnesses of rock and uneven height of the land. Tall cliffs and resistant ledges stand out as headlands, while bays are scooped from softer land behind. Land is only half the story; the sea, too, comes in different shapes and sizes. At Compton each breaking wave has force enough to rake sand back into a long incline, where breakers form a good way out – to the delight of surfers. Ryde is shallow and sandy for different reasons: in the shadow of the Island, sheltered waters deliver more sand than they carry away. Sand itself is just a transitional stage, midway between rock and silt in the endless cycle of erosion and deposit. Each handful of sand contains on average 250 million grains (check it and see). At present there is sand on beaches around a quarter of the Island coastline. But sand is not everything. The small stones at Blackgang, for example, are smooth as peas, warm in summer and comfortable as a bean-bag. They just don't make very good castles.

Beach-cleaning. Council teams do it, Greens do it, even £50,000 machines do it . . . and still the beaches stand testimony to the grim harvest of the sea. Worst in winter, plastic, tar and less visible unpleasantnesses litter the strand.

Council efforts are mainly in summer. Sandown Bay and Ryde Sands are ploughed daily in season by tractor and litter-gathering machine. On council-run beaches where cost and terrain rule out such machines (Cowes, Freshwater . . .), contractors clear litter by hand, while local beach-operators work to keep their own patches clean. Each spring fire-brigade and council teams combine in a beachsweep to tackle areas not included in routine borough beach-cleaning programmes. This work is strongly supported by voluntary efforts throughout the year. Residents' Associations, schools, youth groups, conservationists, pressure-groups – all make regular forays. But improvements are short-lived.

Litter. National surveys suggest beach-litter is 40% land-derived. Not so locally: almost all the rubbish on Island beaches clearly comes from the sea — boating-debris and containers with foreign labels. The worst accumulations are in corners least visited (like Watershoot Bay) and where prevailing winds keep land-derived litter away from beaches. Like a mini-roundabout in the marine highway of the Channel, the Island collects litter from the passing traffic. Beaches seem worst at high water, when the only place to walk is along the narrow strip piled with the dismal deliveries of previous tides.

Dumping at sea of plastic and similar waste was finally made illegal in 1989. As yet there are few signs of the law's success. Almost indestructible, ocean plastic travels 12 miles a day, clockwise, on an everlasting circuit, till trapped by land or wildlife. Worldwide, up to 2 million birds and 100,000 animals are killed each year by marine litter. Britain gets through 5 billion plastic bottles a year; these make up a quarter of the volume of domestic refuse. Bottles and cans gather on Island beaches like hens come home to roost. (It was an I.O.W. firm in the 1930s that first put beer in cans, with yachting-folk in mind).

Winter is the worst time for oil and tar on local beaches. There are 27,000 tanker-dockings each year in British ports. With Fawley Refinery on its doorstep, the Island has reason to be well-prepared for emergencies; some of the world's leading technology for dealing with oil-disasters is Isle of Wight-based. However, two-thirds of oil spilt comes not from accidents that hit the headlines but from routine swilling out of tanks and bilgewater discharges out in the Channel, doing untold harm to sea-life. Unseen pollutants: independent monitoring has consistently shown local radiation levels to be within natural variations and acidity below the national average. But TBT, even in the tiniest quantities, has been shown to have dire consequences for marine life. So much for anti-fouling.

Awards. Concern for the state of beaches and bathing-waters has spawned a bewildering number of award-schemes in recent years. Chief of these is the EC Blue Flag, which as yet (1993) no Island beach has achieved. Confusingly, Ryde East, Springvale and St Helens can fly blue-and-yellow flags as successful entrants in the Tidy Britain Group's Seaside Awards for 1992. Nine Island beaches in the same year entered the Solent Water Quality Awards and all gained plaques — Yaverland, Shanklin North, Totland Bay, Sandown, Shanklin, Colwell Bay, East Cowes, Ryde East, St Helens.

BATHING

Where best to bathe is a matter of personal preference. Those who favour safe waters on sandy beaches stand most chance of satisfaction in the main resorts, where you can usually bathe at most states of tide. In general, the Island is none too good for bathing at low tide. Along much of the northern coast sand gives way to mud; at Foreland, Seagrove and from Brighstone to Freshwater, platforms of rock and slippery ledges are exposed. Where there is plenty of sand (Ryde, Bembridge Point), the water is warm and good for paddling, but you have a long way to splash before it's over your knees. Colder waters but lively waves, often good for surfing, are to be had along the less crowded SW coast. Hurst Narrows, by Ft Victoria, and harbours, piers and navigation channels are places where bathing is strictly prohibited.

Water quality. Time was when people went bathing for the good of their health. Nowadays no one is quite so sure. Concern over the state of our seawater has brought mounting confusion. But research is still in its infancy. At a practical level, improvements in waste-water disposal cannot be achieved over-night. Our muck must all go somewhere. To renew the infrastructure of water works and drains is a colossal undertaking, possible only in phased developments spread over years. Finally, the whole concept of 'clean seas' may be misleading. Seawater in its natural state is a complex cocktail, hardly pure and healthgiving. Unless chemically sterilized, seawater will always contain things to upset bathers.

Since Victorian times Britain has flushed 300 million gallons of raw or barely treated sewage water down short outfalls into the sea each day. By 1975 European waters had got bad enough for laws to be passed enforcing checks and action. Almost two decades on, things are now changing fast. A £3 billion clean-up is in progress. Solent waters are improving. Southern Water is spending £3 million a week till the end of the century on a massive programme of renewal. Schemes have been completed at Sandown, Norton, Gurnard, Ryde and Cowes; Totland is currently being dug up and other works are in the pipeline for Bembridge, St Helens, Ventnor, Freshwater, Colwell and Yarmouth (all due for completion by the EC deadline of 1995). These measures are bringing gradual, if patchy, improvements in water-test results. The irregularities owe much to the weather, with sudden storms or heatwaves messing up the pattern of a season's testing.

In future waste-water schemes will have to conform to stricter standards than hitherto applied. Marine treatment relies on natural forces to deal with sewage — dilution by seawater, dispersal by tide, destruction of bacteria by the sun's ultra-violet rays. Until recently, short outfalls were held to blame for polluted bathing-waters and long outfalls seem to be the answer. Critics felt this was a bit like trying to solve industrial air-pollution by building taller chimneys. New EC directives require additional treatment of marine discharges from urban areas (including the new long outfalls at Ryde and Cowes) by 1998. This is the deadline also for the cessation of sludge-dumping at sea (practised now only by

Britain). A quarter of a million tonnes a year is dropped, controversially, into the Nab Spoil Area. Claimed to be harmless, this practice may yet be linked with the abundance of algal blooms (white foam and unpleasant-smelling brown scum, often mistaken for raw sewage, on the surface of summer seas).

Water-testing. The National Rivers Authority, as an independent body, carries out water-tests around the Island over 22 weeks from May to September. Samples are taken from 13 EC-designated bathing-beaches and 10 'unofficial' beaches where people bathe. 95% of the weekly samples must meet the required standard for a beach to 'pass' in any year. As well as testing for the presence of coliform bacteria, the NRA carries out more than a dozen other checks (phenols, oils, turbidity etc). The NRA has an open-door policy, welcoming enquiries (0983 820692) and encouraging local authorities to display test-results. Several Island resorts now have such notice-boards. To pass EC tests, British waters have only to reach a minimum standard. There is an additional guideline standard, twenty times stricter, adopted by some countries (such as Italy) and beyond the reach of most British beaches. Public notices put water-results in three grades: green star (excellent, EC Guideline Standard), green dot (good, EC Minimum Standard), red dot (poor/fail, Below EC Standards).

SAFETY

There is no such thing as a safe beach, and the following is only a guide.

HAZARDS IN THE WATER

Currents: where these are strongest (Ft Victoria and river channels), bathing is clearly prohibited. Elsewhere currents are not usually a problem for the ordinary bather, though a danger to those ranging further out on sailboards or small craft – especially if swept round headlands like Dunnose or by Castlehaven.

Steep shelving beaches: shingle 'storm' beaches occur on exposed sections, where large stones get shunted up the shore and loose gravel is pulled out from underneath. The result – as at Chale and in corners of Ventnor, Freshwater and Alum Bays – is a steep, unstable bank, which can give a nasty surprise to any paddler. Swimmers, too, should be wary of the undertow or backdraught in such spots – enough to knock one over and drag a body some distance underwater. At Blackgang, even on a seductively calm day and where the beach shelves gently, the force of the breaking wave has been enough to claim lives.

Winds: the prevailing sou-westerlies can be a problem in Sandown Bay, where offshore breezes are the commonest cause of people getting into difficulties (mainly with air-beds and inflatables not held on ropes). When contrary winds meet strong running tides, the sea is whipped up to rough conditions and the red flags are hoisted in Sandown Bay (perhaps half a dozen times a season).

Boating: boat-owners have a duty to be aware of local restrictions in seaside areas. Equally, bathers must stay clear of jetties and recognised access-points for boats and jet-skis. Seagrove, Gurnard and Shanklin have seen problems of this ilk.

Underwater obstructions: each season the local casualty department deals with a steady flow of minor injuries sustained on beaches. The best advice is to have plasters and antiseptic in your beach-bag and to keep something on your feet along the shore. Keep clear of groynes and breakwaters, which are always slippery on top and likely to have debris on one side, a big drop on the other.

Weever fish: in 1991 at least 50 bathers needed First Aid treatment for weever stings in Sandown Bay – sometimes up to 4 or 5 a day. The lesser weever fish comes inshore after shrimps, especially in hot weather and along shallow sandy stretches, as at Ryde and Sandown. It lies buried in the sand and reacts sharply to being trod on, delivering a painful sting from venomous sacs along its black spiny fin. Tradition has it that the pain and swelling will not subside until the tide has turned twice. The only precaution is shoes on your feet.

HAZARDS ON LAND

Cliff-falls: no doubt the greatest danger round the Island, though easy to ignore. Except where pinned back around Sandown/Shanklin, all the cliffs are loose, unstable and liable to sudden falls. This can happen in any season and in any weather, without warning. It is most common – and most alarming – in the Lower Greensand sections of the S.W. coast. GIVE ALL CLIFFS A WIDE BERTH.

Mudflows: while sandstone tends to drop when undercut, clays ooze and flow beneath a beguiling crust of weathered surface. Over the years people have had to be rescued from such mudflows, notably by Blackgang, Atherfield, Brighstone and Bouldnor, as well as from tenacious clays around Thorness.

Rocks: large, slippery boulders impede progress round parts of the coast (Node's Point, Culver, St Lawrence, Rocken End...) and it is not uncommon for people to be caught out by rising tides or injured ankles – with helicopter assistance needed in remote spots. Stout footwear, maps and tidetables are advised.

Shells: live shells and ammunition are still uncovered on Island beaches, part of the legacy of the last war. Do not, as happened recently, drive your discovery round to the police for their opinion. Use the emergency phone to give police the exact location of your suspicious find. The same goes for canisters and drums washed ashore, most often in winter. These should not be touched, in whatever state, but should be reported at once on 999.

Other hazards: oiled sea-birds (these need careful handling, phone RSPCA with precise whereabouts); jellyfish (mostly harmless, though larger species can still sting when dead); sunburn and the harmful effects of unregulated sunbathing; seafront traffic; thefts of valuables from unattended bags.

SAFETY PROVISIONS

Local authorities have to ensure that beaches accessible to the public are covered by a rescue service, but there is no legal requirement to provide lifeguards or a specified level of safety equipment. In a typical year 45 people drown off British beaches. Do-as-you-please Britain, does in the main without lifeguard supervision and complicated flag-systems. The conditions which call for the Red Flag are precisely those most favoured by surfers and sporting types. The Red Flag system carries no powers of enforcement.

Nonetheless, the Isle of Wight does try to prevent and prepare for any emergency. Firstly this means warning-signs, where necessary, and lifebelts and emergency phones (all regularly checked) at each main beach. The phones put one in touch with the coastguard, who co-ordinate rescues, maintain patrols and are trained to deal with all manner of incident – typically dogs over cliffs. (They would rather find just Fido dangling, not his owner too).

Quickest, though not cheapest, of the rescue services may be the Lee-on-Solent helicopter, which can reach all of the Island in 3 to 12 minutes. Bembridge and Yarmouth lifeboats are each called out on average 30-40 times a year, often in the worst possible conditions. Together they save at least a couple of dozen lives a year. Alongside the RNLI are further voluntary units, in the form of inshore rescue teams operating out of Cowes, Ryde, Sandown, Freshwater and Lepe.

In Sandown Bay there is a beach safety service (May-Sept, daily around 9.30-5.30) responsible for monitoring conditions, raising and lowering the Red Flag and keeping a watch over people in the sea. Those involved have lifeguard-training, radio-links with rescue-craft and close contact with HM Coastguard. First-Aid Posts are at Ryde (Arena & Lifeguards HQ), Sandown & Shanklin Esplanades.

REFRESHMENTS

Where two or three are gathered by the sea, there is usually someone not far off ready to sell them an ice-cream. This rule breaks down somewhat between Yarmouth and Cowes. Ice-cream booths and burger-vans are transitory by nature (chips that pass in the night) and the ratings in this guide give just a rough indication as to the availability of food and drink, without judging its quality.

For those who think beaches are best seen over the rim of a teacup or through the base of a beer-glass, the Island has some splendidly situated pubs and tearooms, from the comfort of which it is easy to enjoy the seaside. The Fisherman's Cottage at Shanklin may be the only one right on a beach, but there is no shortage of scenic alternatives poised on cliffs or just yards from the sea.

LOOS

Given its dependence on tourism (2 million visitors claimed each year), the Isle of Wight does not have a lot to offer its visitors when nature calls. Other places seem to manage better. EC requirements on beach standards are bringing gradual improvements – Gurnard, Cowes, Ryde (all in Medina). Elsewhere facilities are often ancient, though the staff who maintain them do well to keep such premises clean and serviceable insofar as possible.

Of public conveniences serving beaches, roughly half stay open all year (though some close at night). The rest are shut from November to March. About a third have disabled units 'open' all year. These are normally separate compartments with an outside door opened with a National RADAR Scheme key.

ENTERTAINMENTS

Punch & Judy and donkeys on the sands have rather given way to space-invaders and the ghetto-blaster. But seaside entertainment is not all dead. Much of it, wisely, has moved indoors – into pubs, theatres and holiday-camps. Free outside entertainments do still flourish in special events each summer. Carnivals (when people appear in funny clothes and behave oddly) and Cowes Week (ditto) are the main such occasions, with other traditional (or pseudo-traditional) festivals, regattas and 'fayres' dotted through the season – invariably on the wettest days of the year. The Isle of Wight is the birthplace of the modern English carnival: Ryde began it all in 1888 and around eight others also continue the August tradition.

Alongside these are sporadic festivities promoted by councils and by local Business & Hoteliers' Associations. Shanklin is the most active in this field, with band-concerts in the gardens and a line-up of morris dancers, jugglers and baton-twirlers in the Old Village. Be there at the right time and you may catch the Punch & Judy.

SPORT

Sailing is the Island's main claim to fame. The great days of Solent yachting belong to the early part of this century, but racing continues most of the year. Beginners can join sailing schools at Cowes (294941), Medina Valley (522195) and Wootton (882246, 882461). Windsurfing/Sail-boarding is enjoyed, not least by spectators, along various points of the north and eastern coastline. Seaview (613222) offers water skiing and rowing-clubs flourish at Newport, Ryde and Sandown/Shanklin. Surfing (club sec. 854010) needs the right conditions, which tend to hit Compton a few days after a deep low in the Atlantic. Hardy swimmers can compete in regatta-events, though few could hope to keep up with Alison Streeter, who in 1984 swam round the Island in the record time of 21 hrs 2 mins. Warmer waters are generally to be found in the Island's 3 indoor pools – Medina (523767), Sandown (405594) and West Wight (752168), where details may be had of local organisations which specialise in scuba/snorkelling/sub-aqua and similar watery sports.

In the air, but still on the coast, parascending is sometimes seen in Sandown Bay and the Solent. W. Wight is home to a successful hang-gliding industry, two world-champions and High Adventure (754042), responsible for kite-men off Compton. Sandown Airport offers pleasure flights, while Bembridge each June hosts the revived Schneider Air Race, originally for seaplanes.

The Island has seven scenic golf-courses, all but one close to the sea. Putting and crazy golf are along almost every sea-front. Bowls has a good following locally, with nine greens in operation, most within a whiff of the sea.

Even at low tide, few Island beaches (apart from Ryde, Bembridge and perhaps Shanklin) have a great deal of space for cricket and football. A small ball is always useful, failing that, try traditional games – marbles, skittles, Treasure Hunt, Matching Pairs, competitions and displays (of stones and shells), building or sculpting castles/people/race-tracks – even mini-Isle of Wights!

HIRE EQUIPMENT

Huts, chairs, windbreaks etc are available in summer along all the main holiday-beaches. On council territory such business is contracted out to beach operators, who take on responsibilities for cleanliness and supervision of their allotted patch. Visitors who, perhaps unaware of these arrangements, question the system or cost of a deckchair, should bear in mind that the concessionaire has paid for rights upon his patch and that such sections are usually the cleanest and safest parts of beach to be found. Today's operators are the descendants – literally in some cases – of the Island longshoremen, who scratched a living 'along shore' in whatever ways season and weather permitted – fishing, boat-repairs, weaving pots, bathing-machines, smuggling. ... Over the years, longshoremen have notched up a fine record in saving lives of those in peril on the sea.

VISITS

Come the rainy day, there are places to visit all over the Island – probably too many for their own good. A few (mainly parks and gardens) have free admission, but the majority of attractions charge, with Osborne House (around £5) perhaps the most expensive. Places of interest are well advertised in free handouts like 'Island Visitor' and 'Holiday News', and further details can be had from Tourist Information Centres (all year at Newport, Ryde, Sandown, Shanklin; in season at Cowes, Ventnor and Yarmouth). It is worth checking ahead on prices and opening-times, especially around either end of the season. Much of the Island shuts up shop for winter.

For summer excursions there are boat-trips out from Yarmouth, Ryde and Sandown Piers, as well as regular cruises from Cowes. Steamers like *Waverley* and *Balmoral* call in most years for special trips. Less glamorous if not always less bumpy are the many coach-tours available within the Island. The classic trip is Round the Island (5½ hours, with stops), always clockwise to avoid locking mirrors.

WALKS

The Island's 600-mile network of public footpaths and bridleways is probably the best signed and most dense per square mile in the country. Trails and coastal path are detailed in leaflets and local publications. The yellow Ordnance Survey map (Outdoor Leisure 29) is ideal for general wandering, while the ITP Guide Map (orange booklet) is strong on footpaths and town-plans.

The Coastal Path goes 67 miles, only just over half of which so far is strictly coastal and footpath. E. Cowes to Fishbourne is the main disappointment. But for 38 miles the path runs close to the sea – sometimes perilously so – making it possible in many parts when the tide is right to complete a pleasant split-level circuit. However, there are few connecting ways between cliff and beach from Rocken End to Brook.

For walking the Island few could hope to beat Pat Gamble, who in 1975 (as a 69 year old, one-armed, ex-bus-conductor on his fifth such circuit) clipped his own record to complete the 65 mile loop in 13hrs 54 mins: probably ahead of his bus.

Accompanied walks are offered by the Ramblers' Association, who always welcome extra feet, while in summer Ranger-led walks (often coastal) are organised by the National Trust and Countryside Management Services, teaming up with local naturalists. For best views, the Island's extremities are the obvious starting-points: Culver, St Catherine's and Needles Headland – all rough and hilly, but relatively dry underfoot. Cowes Front, at the fourth point of the compass, is urban and flat, but always interesting. Likewise Yarmouth and Bembridge Harbours, though hazardous with traffic. Safer are the many esplanades and sea-walls round the Island, giving level sections of coast which wheel- and push-chair users can enjoy.

GEOLOGY

It's odd to think we have Africa largely to thank for the geological splendours of the Isle of Wight. More than 200 million years ago, when the continents broke up, Africa drifted free from S. America and swung up into Europe with a crunch that gave us the Alps. Europe's mountains rose like a rucked-up carpet in ridges and waves, the outer ripples of which are England's North and South Downs. Without this shunt, no doubt Wight would have stayed dully flat and disappeared beneath the waves off Hampshire. Instead the land rose, folded into downland and hardened formations to outwit the sea. Only The Needles and Old Harry Rocks remain of the chalk ridge that once joined Wight with Dorset.

From the white cliffs and softer clays fall the fossils that first excited Victorian scientists. Pioneers swiftly realised the Island's importance and the place has been a happy hunting-ground for geologists ever since. The Island is 'one of the richest sources of dinosaur bones in Europe'. Such claims are not exaggerated, nor are the superlatives confined to dinosaurs. Sites like Hamstead and Whitecliff Bay provide geological exposures which for their scale or completeness are virtually unique.

The Island's rocks are not especially old, but they are of an interesting age, coinciding, as some do, with the heyday of the dinosaurs. The oldest exposed, the Wealden Marls, go back some 120 million years, – which is nothing in geological terms. Geological time is very confusing: what is but a whisker away geologically is eternities off in human terms. If the 4,700 million years since the earth's crust formed are thought of as one year, then it is mid-December before the dinosaurs appear. On this scale, Wight became an island (some 7-8,000 years ago) only in the last 45 seconds.

All the Island's rocks are sedimentary, laid down under water of varying depths and conditions, from warm deep seas (chalk) to freshwater swamps and sub-tropical lagoons (Wealden and Eocene). Deposits formed in shallow coastal waters are now cut back and uncovered in shallow coastal waters. Distinctions are blurred at the water's edge, where fossilized shellfish and crustaceans rub shoulders with their modern counterparts. Life began in the sea; sponges and jellyfish are ten times older than the dinosaurs.

The best starting-point for any fossil-hunter is the Geology Museum at Sandown, where a representative selection of local finds is on display and copies of the Geologists' Code are available. Do not ignore considerations of safety and law elaborated elsewhere in this guide.

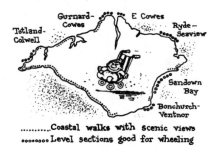

.........Coastal walks with scenic views
oooooooo Level sections good for wheeling

Britain, at the meeting-point of waters from three temperature-zones, has an interesting mix of marine life; but as a well-populated area in a busy part of the world, Wight cannot compete with the remoter isles for spectacles of Nature. Seals are a rarity and penguins even rarer – that seen on Sandown beach, disappearing into the dark pursued by police, was almost certainly a guillemot. What this coastline does have is an abundance and diversity of less exotic, but no less splendid, natural forms – wading-birds on the mudflats, flowers on the chalk cliffs, shells on the beach – enough to give even the least knowledgeable spotter something of interest at any time of year.

Actual marine-life is more elusive. Nature thrives best in a stable home, as on the sheltered shoreline of the Solent. Along the Back of the Wight pounding seas and shifting gravel beaches give fewer footholds for plants and animals. All beaches teem with life and the sea brims with creatures, but most are too small for us to see. Each acre of sea has 10 tons of plankton, the baseline of a mighty food-chain of interdependent species. In this world of stomachs and jaws most creatures depend for survival upon their ability not to be spotted. Add to this the rigours of the elements to which the seashore is exposed (extreme heat and cold, water and desiccation, changes in salinity and seas battering the foreshore with a force of several tons per square foot) and it is small wonder that most marine-life stays tucked up well below your feet or out to sea. A visit to Ft Victoria Aquarium or the Sea Life Centre in Portsmouth may seem one's best hope for encounters with the deep, though debris from the depths is cast up by every tide.

Seashore life divides according to habitat – mud, sand, stones or rock. Down every beach nature is arranged in bands, from splash zone to sub-littoral, in line with the proportion of air to water that each species best enjoys. Thus wracks are found in descending order: spiral, bladder, knotted, serrated . . . Storms foul up these neat arrangements, scattering oarweed and kelp torn from deeper waters and given splendid names – dabberlocks, sea-belt, furbelows and thongweed. Hornwrack, commonly washed up, is something of a curiosity. At first sight ordinary seaweed bleached fawn, on closer inspection it appears to be man-made fabric or a miniature honeycomb. Hornwrack is not seaweed but a cluster of tiny creatures, one of the forms of Bryozoa ('moss-animals') that colonise the sea.

Picked over by rock pipit and wagtail, the vegetation of the strandline may harbour 'mermaid's purses', which are the egg-cases of dogfish (cream, with twirling ends) or skates and rays (dark and horned). Also common are the spongy clusters of egg-capsules from the common whelk, as well as cuttlefish-bones (boil and dry before giving to budgies). The 'bone' is in fact the internal shell of the 'fish' which is a mollusc. Commonest now of Solent shells is the slipper limpet. Introduced by accident from America in the 1890s, the slipper limpet has a pinkish-brown claw-shaped shell, often found attached to another. And another. Changing sex as it grows, the slipper limpet forms one big happy chain of supportive relationships. Its Latin name is *crepidula fornicata*.

HISTORY

'History' may not be the best word to head this section, as many of the most interesting finds from the past around the coastline date back to before the era of written records. Typical of these are the discoveries made by archaeologists beneath the W. Solent, where Stone Age hunters roamed long before the sea broke in. All round the Island evidence of the past drops on to beaches or is uncovered by the waves. Cliffs and shoreline serve as a ready-made dig, constantly eroding back to reveal artefacts that are in fact spread through the whole surface of the Island, like currants in a cake.

'Beach' and 'seaside' are modern concepts, dating back two centuries. Victoria's reign was the Isle of Wight's heyday, when railways and new laws on working-conditions enabled people at large to have holidays, do day-trips and discover the seaside. New towns like Shanklin and Ventnor grew up almost overnight, as the holiday-trade boomed and villas spread, many of them modelled on Osborne.

Before holidaymaking, the history of the coastline is interwoven with tales of smuggling, shipwreck, piracy and rescue, but the dominant theme is defence. Before bathing and leisure, beaches were seen as landing-points for invaders. There is hardly a beach on the Island not overlooked by the remains of some battery, fort or military lookout. Masts and wires from Niton to Ventnor are heirs to the hilltop beacons of Edward III. Because of its strategic position, the Island has always been a tempting target for raiders, from Saxon pirates to Nazi bombers. In 1588 the Spanish Armada and English fleet blew noisily past, exchanging much fire but inflicting no injury. Their relief was short-lived. In 1599, as in 1915 and other occasions, rumours spread that the Island had been taken.

Jumpiness reached a climax in Napoleonic times, leading the government to embark on a massive scheme of fortifications for the Solent approaches. Palmerston's Follies still dominate the scenery to either end of the Island. The various forts were never tested to the full. The Needles Battery did kill one man and half-sink a small boat in 1915: sadly it was one of our own. Likewise the Spithead forts, whose guns only once turned on a French warship – in 1940, when France was our ally.

In the end it was tourists who overran the Island. Victoria came for peace and quiet; ditto Tennyson, and all the world followed. The list of residents and visitors to Victoria's Island reads like a Who's Who to the 19th century – Dickens and Darwin, Garibaldi, Marconi, Karl Marx and Winston Churchill (both treated by the same doctor in Ventnor). Royalty swept in, from Tsar Nicholas and the Kaiser right down to Queen Emma of the Sandwich Isles. Poets, painters, scientist, photographers – all came to see and be seen. Like shipping movements, the arrivals and departures of noteworthy guests were proudly circulated by hotels and papers in each resort. By the 1920s the spell was wearing thin; it was a new age and arty folk were keen to move out of the shadows of the Victorian past. France was discovered, later Spain, and once again all the world followed, leaving Isle of Wight hoteliers and landladies to struggle ever since.

RATINGS

Stars in the Bucket

An element of assessment and grading has deliberately been included in this guide, but inevitably such ratings are subjective. The Stars in the Buckets are a quick guide to the overall quality of each beach. The ratings take into account the entire coastline shown in the section-map, together with its amenities, on a year-round basis, and not just its strip of sand in summer.

modest   **variable**   **good**   **recommended**   **best of all**

Graded Symbols

These indicate the character of each beach and the range of amenities available within a reasonable distance. Each aspect (Access, Beach, Bathing etc.) of every coastal section has been graded and the result shown by the 'watermark' or amount of background filled in (the blacker the better) behind each boxed symbol. See example below.

   non-existent
                        none

   fair
                        average

   poor
                        few

   good
                        plenty

   moderate
                        some

   excellent
                        abundant

Abbreviations

HT, HW	high tide, high water	NT	National Trust
LT, LW	low tide, low water	EC	European Community
IWCC	Isle of Wight County Council	SWA	Southern Water Authority
MBC	Medina Borough Council	NRA	National Rivers Authority
SWBC	South Wight Borough Council	SSSI	Site of Special Scientific Interest

EAST COWES
Poor beach, grand viewpoint.

Access. Easy as far as it goes. Step straight out of your car and into the sea as far as Old Castle Point; beyond that it's private property all the way to Wootton. Car-parking free along the Esplanade. *Buses*: service 5 from Newport or 4 from Ryde – get out before it crosses on the Floating Bridge.

Beach. Best appreciated from a car parked by the sea-wall with the windows up – that way you can enjoy the views of Solent shipping without having to catch the pong of seaweed below. The foreshore here, known as The Shrape, has a long-standing problem with seaweed. Predominant currents, backed by onshore winds, push weed and litter into corners without escape. The half-mile seafront, built in stages as 1920s unemployment relief, makes a pleasant promenade; removal of shingle for 19th century ship-ballast is given as one reason for loss of beach below. Meanwhile plans are mooted for the 21st century, involving land-reclamation and a marina. The long breakwater divides river from sea: inside it is mud, old tyres and the occasional bait digger. Beyond the breakwater, silt turns to shingle with more prominent rocks exposed at low tide. The best chance of sandy patches is along from the playground. Beach and road end abruptly by the ruins of a summer house belonging to Norris Castle.

Bathing. Once a prime spot, with bathing-machines and, later, diving-pontoons, but not a place now really to recommend for swimming. Doubts arise over water-quality, with reports locally of sewage-pollution. Yet the beach has achieved a 100% pass-rate in NRA tests for the last five years.

Safety. Safe enough, if you keep off the breakwater and out of the harbour mudflats. Cowes Rescue is close at hand and, if it's any comfort, the RNLI Inshore Lifeboat centre at East Cowes is a servicing and development depot of worldwide importance.

Refreshments/Loos. Picnic area and small cafe/kiosk in season; failing that, it's the drinking-fountain, newly restored. Well supplied with loos, with a new block near Westlands and a more ancient predecessor beyond. Disabled unit at Town Hall (Osborne Road).

Entertainment. Carnival processions and events in August. Also, a safe distance from which to view Fireworks Night and other Cowes Week revels.

Sport. Children's playground and paddling-pool; tennis-courts (with kit for hire). Golf at Osborne (295421) in regal surroundings. Castle Point is favoured by anglers, hoping for bass, mullet and flatfish, according to season.

Visits. Osborne House (200022) is the obvious attraction, with nearby Barton Manor (292835) also of interest, though the house itself is not open. Once part of Osborne, the Barton Estate now serves the noble grape, producing wines that have found their way into Harrods, the Ritz and Buckingham Palace. Prince Albert's church at Whippingham completes the circuit. Preserved in aspic since the old queen died and long before – she gave orders that nothing be changed or thrown away – Osborne reeks of widowhood and mourning in all its corridors and draughty staterooms. (Victoria never felt the cold, to the dismay of all around her). The estate ran on a clockwork of rituals; when the queen was in residence, Highland cattle had to appear in view from her windows. The house is a clutter of small memorials. But there was another Osborne, alive and sunny, busy with the sound of growing children, which was, for Victoria at least, 'a perfect paradise'. Here she bathed from rickety contraptions,watched her family play on the beach and heard out the complaints of the royal tutor (the Prince of Wales 'made faces and spat'). Here, too, Albert toiled ('like a donkey in Carisbrooke'), planned improving works and one night in the grounds, while listening for nightingales, was arrested by an over-zealous constable.

Walks. Limited. From Old Castle Point eastward for the next three miles the foreshore is strictly private with no unauthorised access. Most once belonged to the Osborne Estate, but is now shared out between Norris Castle, Osborne House, Barton Manor and other owners further east. Along the bay are several historic buildings used first by royal beachgoers, then by convalescent officers and finally abused by vandals and intruders, necessitating a high level of security. Hence, perhaps, the sign which reads 'Patients are warned there are poisonous snakes in the wood'. There are moves to open up a public footpath along the coast. Edward VII did give Osborne to the nation – he was glad to be shot of it – and it's not much of a coastal footpath along the back-roads to Wootton. Maybe nature and posterity are best served by keeping Osborne Bay private, leaving it to curlew and grebe. Beach users are not missing out. Time, tide and wartime manoeuvres have done for the Bay, much of which is in a state of natural dereliction. Groynes, pier and a good deal of sand have gone, leaving boulders, weed and patches of clay.

Natural History. Osborne takes its name ('Austerbourne') from the oyster-beds along the Peel and Mother Banks, which are still fished today, though the season is brief. Coldest winter brings in waders and wildfowl to feed on the crustaceans and eel-grass that colonise the Shrape. Brent Geese come down from the Arctic and grey plover in from Siberia; both must feel pleasantly at home in East Cowes when the wind is a fresh north-easterly.

24

History. East Cowes is a misnomer. Pedants note: technically it's East Cow and West Cow, together making Cowes. But no one can agree whether 'cow' meant fort or sandbank – or just a term of abuse between the rival settlements. Late in the 18th century Norris Castle was built, in mock-medieval style, and then East Cowes Castle, the 'gingerbread Gothic' fantasy John Nash created for himself. The castle was demolished in the 1950s; all that remains is the ice-house in Sylvan Lane, preserved for bats. Nash – architect of Regent Street, Brighton Pavilion, Buckingham Palace and St James' Church, E.Cowes – died with vast debts. His coffin was hurried across fields by night, to foil creditors planning to arrest the corpse. When, by contrast, Victoria's coffin passed silently through the crowds lining Beatrice Avenue in 1901, E.Cowes ceased to be centre of the known world – for such it must have seemed to residents used to emperors passing through and ministers heading up the hill to surrender or receive their seals of office. Outshone now by its classier neighbour, East Cowes still makes its mark through pioneering industries in marine and aerospace concerns. Westland's Union Jack, saved over from the Silver Jubilee, claims to be the largest in the world.

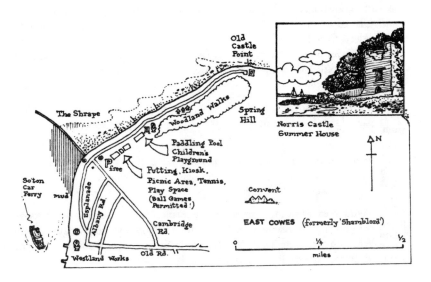

WOOTTON
WOODSIDE

Quiet shoreline alongside abandoned holiday village, nervously awaiting future development.

 Access. Far from immediate. By car, negotiate the potholes, ruts and somewhat superfluous force of sleeping policemen along so-called New Road. (It is due to be re-built as part of an impending development scheme.) Where the road meets others and turns private, there is room to leave just a car or two, before following the path (N 156) which brings you out by the sea in just a few minutes. Plenty of *buses* through Wootton (1A, 1B, 1C and others), but still a good mile and a bit to the sea.

Beach. By Warner's site the beach consists of a narrow band of sand and stones, with a line of shingle and blown sand above and, at low tide, a large expanse of mud below. In both directions progress is soon impeded by mud and weed, loose rock and fallen trees. Towards Wootton Creek are fossil shells and occasional bits of alligator and turtle, which once inhabited the lagoons now turned to coloured clays within the Osborne Beds. Back the other way, beyond the cafe, private land and foreshore run down to high-water mark, with the privately owned nature reserve at King's Quay tucked in behind. False legend has it that King John came here to sulk after signing Magna Carta, however the nearby cottage did house Queen Victoria's gamekeeper. From Woodside the view extends over 4 miles of water to Lee-on-Solent. In between lies Peel Bank, the wartime anchorage of Mulberry harbour, 2 million tons of concrete and steel, which played a critical part in the Normandy landings. Bits still lie scattered about. Along from King's Quay is Barton Hard, with Osborne Bay just round the corner. In Tudor times this was Mead Hole, the venue by all accounts of a kind of mass car-boot sale for smuggled goods and things that slipped off the back of a galleon.

 Bathing. Unattractive underfoot, except at high tide. Water-quality has passed standard tests over the last five years. Safety: reasonable.

 Facilities. Seasonal facilities all concentrated in the Woodside Beach Bar & Cafe – beer garden, food, children's play area, (parking & loos for patrons only) – a well-hidden but enterprising concern, which deserves to succeed.

Visits. Nearest attractions some way inland. Worth checking when trains are running, if planning to visit the recently extended Havenstreet-Wootton Steam Railway (882204). Butterfly World at Wootton (883430) has much to recommend it, not least its warmth.

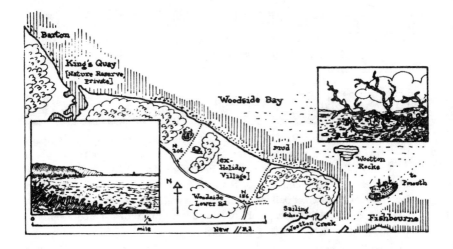

Natural History. An SSSI with red squirrel in the woods and divers and grebe to be spotted out in the bay in winter. The (private) woodland by King's Quay is called Curlews Copse and the foreshore often rings to the curlew's distinctive cry.

History. In Nelson's time the view from Woodside was of a forest of masts, 'the wooden walls of England'. Things have changed a bit since 1841, when the village of Wootton was deemed 'one of the prettiest in the island'. It is now something of a sprawl along the busy Ryde-Newport corridor. The creek is still attractive, while only time will tell what may become of the derelict beach at Woodside. Plans exist for a £50 million marina and time-share development.

SALT

Seawater round Britain is just over 3% salt. With two-thirds of the world covered by sea, more than 6 miles deep in places, there's enough salt in the oceans to spread over the land 500 ft thick. It would take some time to do, though. Getting salt from seawater is a slow but simple process, as any child with a shallow dish, a sunny window-sill and sufficient patience will tell you. 200 years ago the Island had 42 pans producing salt, much in demand for the navy's pork. Those at Newtown were worked till the 1880s, by which time salt came more cheaply from the ground in Poland or Cheshire. Seawater contains other minerals in solution besides salt – phosphates, nitrates, sulphates of sodium, potassium, calcium, magnesium, traces of tin, zinc, chromium, gold (enough in every 100 tons to make a sovereign) and silver (13 million tons of it). Silvery seas indeed.

FISHBOURNE/BINSTEAD

Wooded coastline, mostly mud and stones, which
tends to guard its privacy somewhat jealously.

 Access. Patchy. Limited to sections between properties with bye-law
backed signs marking out 'private land, beach and foreshore to low-water
mark'. Beyond the ferry-terminal, Fishbourne Lane runs down to a small
patch of shore. The backwoods of Binstead (off Church Road) provide further
opportunities for discreet parking, before taking marked footpaths (R 46 or 47) to
the shore. As with Wootton, plenty of *buses* ply the main road (1A,B,C), but you
still have a fair walk to the sea.

 Beach. Very little beach as such. From Wootton to Ryde the muddy
foreshore at low water is dug over by fishermen after fat, brick-red rag-
worm prized as bait. A certain amount of blown sand at the top of the
shore, succeeded by rough stony patches, with mottled clays (red, green, blue)
poking through. Even in this most sheltered part of the Island coastline, away
from SW winds and Channel swell, the sea gives proof of its powers of erosion.
From Osborne to Ryde, in the quiet conditions of the Solent, the foreshore is
punctuated by the fallen remains of trees that once fringed the water's edge.
Sucked out by the tide and clasped by mud, these skeletons are in the first stages
of fossilization, results of which can be seen, 115 million years on and ten miles
off, spilling out of the Island by Brighstone and Brook.

 Bathing. Try Ryde. 19th century maps show a Bathing Pond at Binstead,
but there is no obvious part of the coast here now which is suitable for
bathing – least of all anywhere near the terminal at Fishbourne.

Refreshments/Loos. Congenial refreshments at the Fishbourne Inn
(882823). Nothing doing for loos, except at the Ferry Terminal (inc. disabled
unit). Otherwise no facilities close to the shore from Wootton to Ryde.

Visits. Brickfields Horse Country (66801) – all year, all weather, all you
could ever wish for to do with horses of every shape and size.

Walks. The coastal path from Fishbourne (R 3) takes in plenty of historical
interest. Monks from France came here to settle in 1131 and again in 1908.
Pass through the stone arch to be alongside the original Quarr abbey, once
fortified against attacks by pirates. Little remains of the buildings, swiped up for
Tudor castles and harbours at Yarmouth and Cowes, as well as for the 18th
century farmhouse incorporated into the back of the new brick Abbey. Here
Victoria's youngest, Princess Beatrice, was allowed off her leash for the briefest of

honeymoons in 1885 – two days in the home of her friend Minnie Cochrane, just about visible from Osborne if the Queen used binoculars. Land round Quarr was bought up by Sir Thomas Fleming, the Lord Chief Justice who tried Guy Fawkes. Large properties, now coyly hidden, were put up in later centuries; dank paths lead through shrubbery where one half expects the ghosts of Victorian ladies to bustle past. The coastal path continues by Binstead Church with graveyard curiosities – a pagan idol and the tomb of Samuel Landon, reputed in 1844 to have been the biggest man in the world.

Geology/Natural History. Quarr and Pitts Lane take their names from the quarries where hard Bembridge Limestone was dug out over many centuries. Much was shipped off Binstead Hard for such buildings as Beaulieu and Romsey Abbeys, Chichester and Winchester Cathedrals. Good winter birdwatching all along this northern coast.

History. Boats have tied up at Fishbourne for thousands of years. Latest in the line are the big, new Super-ferries, whose manoeuvring wash has swept the adjoining private beach to expose an archaeological site rich in finds. 3,000 year-old oaks, 2,000 year-old flint tools, sea defences from 500 BC, Roman pottery, medieval cargo … The sea off Binstead is marked on old maps as Quarantine Grounds. A century back two hulks were parked here to take cases of cholera and malaria from ships heading into Southampton. In fact the hulks had not been used as such for 20 years; but they stayed, in deference to the Queen, who felt they added to the view from Osborne.

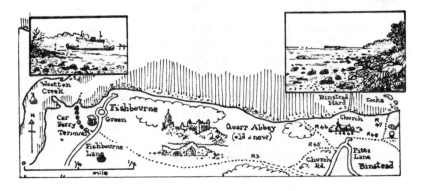

RYDE WEST

Not much at high water, but low tide reveals a good expanse of clean sand.

Access. Easy at first. Step on to the beach at Western Gardens, just left of the pier, and continue west along the lower shore. Surprisingly, there is no further public access on to the sands in this direction until Binstead, a legacy of the large estates that first made up this part of Ryde. Along Pelham-fields private frontages still extend down to the high-tide mark. No shortage of *buses* (most of the Island's public transport begins or ends here); three large (pay) car-parks close at hand – off St Thomas' Street and around the Ice Rink.

Beach. Good in the late afternoon sun, which it catches. The beach is mostly flat; the pier is almost half a mile – just a bit further than the tide goes out, leaving a sizeable area of firm, wet sand. Soft, dry and less clean sand is confined to the corner by the pier, which can get very crowded when the tide is up. Dog-free zone in season for 100 metres seawards. The beach looks north-west to Calshot (8 miles off) and ahead over 3½ miles of busy water to Gosport. There's plenty to watch with catamarans and pilot-boats buzzing about the pierhead. The 10p telescope on the front somewhat optimistically gives distances to the planets.

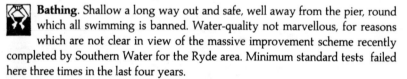

Bathing. Shallow a long way out and safe, well away from the pier, round which all swimming is banned. Water-quality not marvellous, for reasons which are not clear in view of the massive improvement scheme recently completed by Southern Water for the Ryde area. Minimum standard tests failed here three times in the last four years.

Safety. Soft clay along the lowest part of the shore has trapped horses and riders in the past, but for the average beachgoer this section is generally clear of hazards. First Aid Post incorporated in the Arena complex.

Refreshments/Loos. All along the Esplanade, but nothing west along the beach. New block of tin and tile (incl. disabled unit) loos tucked away behind the Information Centre – and not a patch on the 1902 marble halls (opened by Princess Beatrice) which it replaced.

Entertainment/Sport. Ryde Front with its rock-shops and Arcadia Amusements has all a small boy could wish for. Ryde Golf Club (614809) is nicely positioned, just up from the beach. Angling from Ryde Pier is now restricted to club members in a designated area, to stop fishermen catching ferries. Deckchairs can be hired from the Western Esplanade.

Visits. Just off Ryde and to the west lies Mother Bank, from where the first settlers set sail for Australia in 1787. Two hundred years on the Queen opened a commemorative exhibition in the redundant St Thomas' Church, where (May-Sept) details are displayed of that historic journey.

Walks. It is a 25 minute low-tide ramble along the foreshore to Binstead, the last part less good going, with mud, weed and rock. Pause by Binstead Point to admire the exquisite ripple-marked sandstone flags which date back 35 million years. The route back inland from Binstead takes a bit longer. Head up Ladies' or Lovers' Walk (same path, different purposes) and cut down through Ryde past large houses (such as Westfield, with stag couchant over the gateway). Ryde developed in the 18th and 19th centuries through the energies of two or three important families (Players, Linds, Brigstockes), who bought, built and inter-married. Older residents still (correctly) call Ryde West 'Player's Beach'.

Natural History. At low-tide the whole beach is coiled with worm-casts, giving just a hint of what goes on beneath the surface. Up to nine inches long and as thick as your finger, the lugworm lies in its U-shaped burrow eating dirt for 5-8 hours a day. Every so often it squirts up its leftovers into a cast about six inches from the small hole where its head end lies.

History. Once 'frequented by the nobility and gentry during the season', Ryde was the 'chosen resort of the elite', where 'dukes and earls took the air on the pier'. Things have changed, no doubt for the better, and Ryde is pleasantly unpretentious, though fine buildings remain as memorials to its former grandeur. The 180 feet spire of All Saints Church (Gilbert Scott) is Ryde's distinctive landmark.

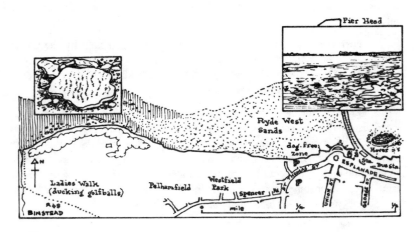

RYDE CENTRAL

Traditional seaside, with all the fun of the fair.

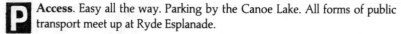

Access. Easy all the way. Parking by the Canoe Lake. All forms of public transport meet up at Ryde Esplanade.

Beach. Flat and sandy. The muddier part has disappeared beneath the new Arena/car park/harbour complex. Large beach-cleaning machine ploughs the sands to good effect. Dog-free zone along the top 100 metres of the beach in season from Cornwall Slip to Appley Tower.

Bathing/Safety. Good, safe bathing with recent improvements in the water quality. No main safety hazards on the beach, but beware of thefts from unattended bags along the seafront.

Refreshments/Loos. Cafes, kiosks, bars and hotels all in abundance. Choice of loos from the station to Eastern Gardens.

Entertainment. All the way along, from the Arena to the Canoe Lake. Centre-stage is the Peter Pan playground, with fairground-type attractions, and things for children. In Eastern Gardens are trampolines and obstacle golf, with intermittent Sunday afternoon band concerts further along. The Arena ice-rink is growing in popularity while the 1920s Pavilion, has ten-pin bowling alongside. The Canoe Lake (pedaloes and canoes) is Sunday venue for members of the Model Yacht Club. The first modern English carnival took place in Ryde in 1888; the next year's parade was watched by Queen Victoria from the Town Hall. The event continues, right at the end of August, with processions, sports, sand-castle competitions and similar. Regattas, rowing and sailing, in May and July.

Sport/Hire. Swimming-pools (main, learner and paddling) by the Canoe Lake – all outdoor, but heated. On the Esplanade are two fine bowling-greens, good for spectators. The white helmeted ladies of the local bowls teams are quite something to be reckoned with.

Walks. A fine, level, if breezy promenade. 'Gateway to the Island', Ryde Esplanade bustles with coaches and cars, boats and trains. Transport-buffs can be in seventh heaven on the wobbly bridge over the railway, with commanding views of buses and hovercraft, while ex-London Underground trains rattle up through your legs from the tunnel behind. Half-day excursions on land or sea can be joined at this point, in the form of Round-the-Island coach-trips and Solent cruises (details in Tourist Information Centre).

Natural History. Wading-birds gather in good numbers over winter on Ryde Sands, – redshank, ringed plover, bar-tailed godwit ... Dunlin fly up in groups that flash white as they turn, while paler sanderlings skitter nervously up and down the strand like overwound clockwork toys.

 History. The battlemented Hotel Ryde Castle was built in Tudor times, by order of Henry VIII, or in 1834 by John Dashwood, according to whom you believe. Either way, it gives fine views over Spithead, scene of Fleet Reviews since the 1400s. The Queen's Silver Jubilee (1977) was the most recent, and that in July 1914 the most momentous. No less poignant was that in 1901, when the diminutive Royal Yacht bearing Queen Victoria's coffin made its way in a shaft of sunlight down the ten-mile corridor of battleships between Cowes and Portsmouth. Crowds gathered on Ryde Front in 1982 to peer at the raising of the *Mary Rose*. The ship foundered in 1545, close enough to Southsea Castle for Henry VIII to hear the cries of his drowning men. Only about 40 of the 700 men aboard escaped, many trapped inside the anti-boarding nets rigged to keep out the French. Caught in a breeze, Henry's flagship simply tilted over enough for the gunports, carelessly left open, to fill with water. 237 years later, on almost the same spot, the same thing happened again. Another flagship, the *Royal George*, sank just before setting sail to relieve Gibraltar. Around 900 were drowned, many of them women and children on board to say goodbye. It was the worst tragedy in local waters and the most stupid. The ship was deliberately heeled over to repair a stopcock below the waterline. A carpenter twice tried to warn a junior officer, but was rebuked for impertinence. Minutes later the ship went down, leaving top-masts to poke through the water and bodies to wash up in Ryde for a long time after.

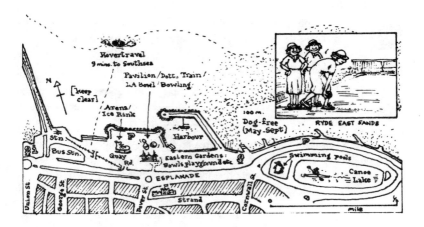

RYDE APPLEY

Popular beach offering good facilities and loads of sand; all that's missing sometimes is the sea.

Access. Good. A pleasant walk along the sea-wall from either direction and free parking close to beach in Appley and Puckpool Parks – in the shade, if you're clever. *Buses*: Service 12 in the summer loops round Ryde to Puckpool.

Beach. Ryde boasts 'six miles of safe and sandy beaches'. More like three and a bit on my map, but perhaps it's mean to quibble about the exact length of the sands, given their width. Off Appley the sands extend more than a mile out to sea, ending with a tapering spit parallel to the shore. ¾ mile east, by Puckpool Point, a second spit, called the Debnigo, runs out in the direction of No Man's Land Fort. Southsea lies 4 miles off over water which is basically shallow – only 6-12 feet at low tide over the shoals of Sturbridge, Horse Sand, Spit Bank and No Man's Land. In the middle is a narrow deep-water channel representing the course of the old Solent River, which flowed out to sea from Southampton when the Island was still part of the mainland and the coast much further away. Generally clean, the beach tails off towards Springvale, with seaweed and litter trapped round Puckpool Point. From the Dell Cafe at Puckpool to a point 200 metres west, the top 100m of beach are dog-prohibited in season.

Bathing. Shallow but warm. Flattish for the most part, the sands get scooped out in places to make hollows for bathing. The large concrete doorway at Appley marks the completion of major new sewage works. Water-quality good.

Safety. It is possible to get cut off here. The tide comes in fast over the sands, masking deeper holes and curling round the back of slightly raised banks. However, the voluntary lifeguards at Appley (Ryde Inshore Rescue) keep a good look out at busy times for just such an eventuality.

Refreshments/Loos. Good cafes at Appley and Puckpool (two). Appley has a 'prestigious new toilet block', pride of the council (summer only). Also loos at Puckpool (both with disabled units).

Entertainment. Children's play area at Appley – Bouncy Castle, sandpit, pirate ship etc. – but they (or rather, you) pay to get in. Free swings and play area at Puckpool, with other modest attractions.

Sport/Hire. Pitch and Putt at Appley. Tennis, bowls, obstacle golf and putting at Puckpool. Deckchairs in between.

 Walks. The sea-wall makes a pleasant promenade. Hidden behind it for the first part is St Cecilia's Abbey, whose Benedictine nuns are known world-wide for their recordings of Gregorian chants. Appley House was built by the smuggler Daniel Boyce, who died a debtor in the Fleet Prison in 1740. The sisters now make their altar-bread in the cellars where Boyce kept his contraband. Walkers on the seafront compete at points with the Dotto Train, a tractorlike vehicle that thinks it's a steam engine. Very small children go free and will enjoy the ride: adults pay.

 Natural History. Should you see paddlers with plastic bags pausing every so often to pick up things below water, it's cockles they're after.

 History. Puckpool Battery, built in 1863 and in commission till 1928, was equipped with mortars to stave off French invasions. Nearby St Clare, now part of Warner's holiday centre, belonged in the last century to Vernon Harcourt, the 'mad professor' claimed by some to have been the inspiration for Lewis Carroll's White Knight. Appley Tower, meanwhile, will have caused many a visitor off the Dotto train to head straight up its fairytale steps, rattle on the locked door and wonder what mysteries lie within. The answer is deckchairs. Built as a folly by a Victorian Paymaster-General, the Disneyesque tower has served in the past as shell museum, tea house and souvenir kiosk. Illuminated at night but closed to the public, it is now a temporary store, while the council awaits happier times financially in which to carry out the repairs needed, before a more suitable use can be found.

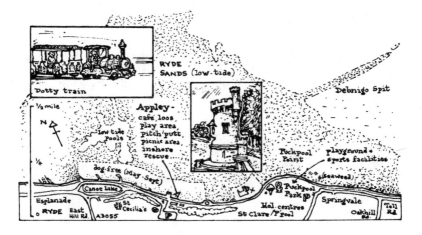

SEAVIEW

Primarily a sailing village, but with some fine, sandy bays, often cited as favourite beaches.

Access. Easy at Springvale, with space for free parking along the sea-wall, and straighforward as far as the Esplanade at Seaview (though visiting cars must pay 20p to make use of the short section of toll-road in between). Thereafter, access becomes more difficult with few places to leave a car within striking distance of the sea. Seagrove and Priory Bays are best reached along the beach from Seaview or St. Helens, or on the Coastal Path through Priory Woods with steps on to the beach.

Beach. *Springvale:* the beach from Puckpool to Nettlestone Point is the continuation of Ryde East Sands, tapering to a point at Seaview. Shingle is banked up against The Duver at projecting points; below this is a fairly level expanse of firm sand, with a certain amount of weed, pebble, rocks and occasional muddy patches. *Dogs* banned (May-Sept) along the top 100m of beach from the Tollgate to the Battery Hotel, Springvale.

Seagrove Bay: rocky offshore for the first part, from Esplanade to Sandcove. Shallow foreshore; clean, safe, family beach with a fair strip of sand at low-tide, turning stonier (and, in some years, muddier) towards Horestone Pt. Dogs banned along top 100m of Sandcove. High-water laps against the wall beneath the new waterside development. Seaview once boasted the undulating Chain Pier (1880-1951), a thousand feet long and almost unique – Brighton had the other one – from which tripper boats, known as 'sixpenny sickers', ran to Southsea.

Priory Bay: except at high-water, a wide band of sand, with low-tide rockpools well-stocked with sea-life. Peaceful beach, backed by trees, with only remnants of sea-wall to show where earlier in the century stood a row of elegant villas. Busy in summer.

Bathing. *Springvale:* paddling and shallow bathing, maybe, but not much of a swim, especially at low-tide. The large tidal range at this end of the Island means that when the tide does rise, it can race in at some speed over the relatively flat sands. Water-tests passed over the last five years and 1992 winner in the rural section of the Tidy Britain Group's Seaside Awards. (Sewage pipes here and in Seagrove Bay are storm outfalls, activated by flood conditions only).

Seagrove Bay: has its advocates, but is not without problems. Water-quality, though currently being tackled, has not been good in recent years. In addition, with its slipways and sheltered waters, the bay has been popular with jet-skiers (now banned) in past summers and this has led to disputes between residents, bathers and participants in conflicting water-sports.

Priory Bay: usually quieter than Seagrove, with some space for shallow bathing in clearish waters, if you avoid the rocks and boats.

 Safety. Safe seas for most of the year off this corner of the Island, the main hazards arising from water-sports. Watch out, too, for slippery conditions around rocks, steps and slipways festooned with algae.

 Refreshments/Loos. Facilities tend to be in Springvale or Seaview itself, with little to the south of the village. For a meal with a view, the Old Fort Inn (612363) will take some beating. Other fare on offer at the Tollgate in Springvale. Beach cafe at Seagrove Bay. Loos are at the Rope Walk, Seaview and Gully Rd, Seagrove (seasonal).

 Entertainment. 3-day Regatta in mid-August, with beach sports, tug o' war and fireworks display 'to rival Cowes'. There are long-standing links between Seaview and Conservative politicians; during the summer recess, the sight and sound of Junior Cabinet Ministers in public-school games-shorts gives the bay a slightly unreal Fifties air, with just a hint of Surrey By The Sea.

 Sport. Seaview Watersports (613222) at Springvale has most things on offer – waterskiing, windsurfing, canoes, sailing, sub-aqua . . . Close by is Puckpool with land-based activities, such as tennis and putting.

 Visits. Flamingo Park (612153, Easter-Oct) is a Local Award-winning at- traction for lovers of Waterfowl and Water-gardens. No dogs allowed. On the site of former salterns, Barnsley Creek was also where oak trees from the Oglander estates were piled up for the dockyards at Portsmouth, ready to be towed across the Solent by convict row-barges.

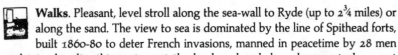 **Walks**. Pleasant, level stroll along the sea-wall to Ryde (up to 2¾ miles) or along the sand. The view to sea is dominated by the line of Spithead forts, built 1860-80 to deter French invasions, manned in peacetime by 28 men and joined earlier this century at the landward ends by a barrage to keep out Germans. They were built of concrete, granite and iron on shallow shoals, with walls more than 14 ft thick. Nearest to Springvale are No Man's Land (1½ miles) and Horse Sand (2¾m); Spit Bank is close to Portsmouth and the fourth, St Helens, lurks round the corner. The view down Seaview High St perfectly frames the newly-painted No Man's Land Fort offered for sale in 1990 at £5¾ million, as a luxury time-share development.

Natural History. Springvale to St Helens is a good section for winter birdwatchers with a chance of seeing divers (if they surface!) and other cold-season visitors – little grebes, red- and black-throated divers, barnacle geese, red-breasted mergansers . . . Below the Esplanade are boulders of Nettlestone Grit, which weather unevenly into hollows much inhabited by winkles, anemones and some very large limpets. Or, to give their scientific name, patellae – which means 'little pans'. Or kneecaps.

History. July 19th 1545 was both the day the *Mary Rose* went down and the last occasion the Island was invaded by a foreign power. Landings were made at four places – Seaview (as commemorated by the plaque on the Esplanade), Bembridge, Sandown and Bonchurch. All were repulsed, which was no mean feat, since the French fleet and invading force (30,000 soldiers, according to one report, aboard more than 230 vessels) were larger than those of the Spanish Armada a generation on. Here also hundreds of vessels gathered in the Solent in early summer of 1944, ready to carry out Operation Overlord. Off Seaview the water was packed with ships, just part of the 5,000 strong fleet mustered for the Normandy Landings. Overnight on 5/6th June, the whole lot vanished. The Longest Day had begun.

Isle of Wight parson

ST HELENS

A few sandy patches, but mainly hollows in which to wallow in glorious mud.

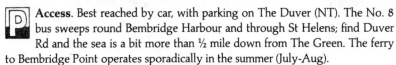

 Access. Best reached by car, with parking on The Duver (NT). The No. 8 bus sweeps round Bembridge Harbour and through St Helens; find Duver Rd and the sea is a bit more than ½ mile down from The Green. The ferry to Bembridge Point operates sporadically in the summer (July-Aug).

Beach. A beach which evokes happy memories of bathing and cockling, but which now resounds more to the squelch and scrape of bait-diggers at work. Sandy patches along the top at either end of The Duver, but, as yet, not a lot of sand in between, where new groynes have been installed for beach-replenishment. South (to the right) of the old church is mostly mud and stones as far as the sandy corner, which soon gives way to harbour-silt. In the other direction, shingle with some sand above low-tide ledges of rock, which build up to a formidable obstruction around Node's Point. Sea-wall and rocky outcrops mean little beach exposed at high-tide around St Helens.

 Bathing. Not marvellous – better places to try in the near vicinity. Unattractive underfoot in the shallows and unsafe further out. Water-quality below par.

 Safety. Take heed of the various signs warning that 'it is dangerous to bathe in the channel due to strong currents'. A steady stream of boats at high-water should also knock on the head any foolish ideas of swimming across the harbour-mouth.

 Refreshments/Loos. Old Church Cafe in season on The Duver. Rather grim seasonal loos alongside the above (incl. disabled unit).

 Entertainment. The village Carnival & Sports, at the end of August, is a traditional knees-up and jollification. (Be warned, though, that beach N of the old church is National Trust property, with bye-laws forbidding bonfires, noise and similar carousing).

 Hire. Windbreaks, beach-huts, caravans ... all from the cafe. The beach huts are old railway-carriages, once the pride of Southern Railway. Former owners of the harbour (and of green-painted sheds around it), the company had notions of turning Bembridge into the main ferry-terminal, should Ryde ever prove non-viable. Instead it was Bembridge which silted up first.

Walks. Interesting rambles in both directions. South is The Duver, leading round to the harbour causeway and site of the old mill. 'Duver' means patch of sandy waste-ground and the name crops up again at Seaview and Ryde. The turf and duneland at St Helens are famous firstly for flowers (a botanist's delight, especially in spring and autumn) and secondly as home till 1961 of the Royal I.W. Golf Club. But the course, packed into too tight an area, with fairways criss-crossing, was reckoned to be 'one of the most dangerous in the world'. Casualties included passing boats, walkers on footpaths and one dead dog. Ways round Node's Point are difficult along the beach, especially if the tide is up. Paths cut through Priory Woods or inland past the Holiday Centre. Warner's (part of Mecca Leisure) have seven sites on the Island; Node's Point can cater for more than 2,000 visitors, in tents and chalets. Beyond is the Priory Hotel. Once farmhouse to the priory, long suppressed, the building was bought in Stuart times by a certain Mr Badd, who was, according to the local diarist, a poor man's son, 'but by God's blessing and ye losse of five wyfes he grew very ritch'.

Natural History. Abundance of birds, flowers and marine-life around St Helens, which concentrates within a small area a rich diversity of habitats – rock-pools, dunes, mudflats ... Also abundant is Japanese Seaweed, one local speciality that the I.O.W. would rather not have had. The first record of attached 'japweed' growing in the North Atlantic was at Bembridge on 17th February 1973, an accidental import into these parts. Japweed grows rapidly in spots like marinas during the summer months, putting on nearly an inch a day to reach lengths of 9ft, choke shallow waters and crowd out other species. The distinctive brown strings with little air-sacs are still much in evidence on Island beaches, despite vigorous efforts over the years to eradicate it. Japanese Seaweed is not the only alien brought in by ships from abroad. The Island is home also to a species of marine-worm from Japan, to a sea-anemone from the Western Pacific and to a barnacle from Australia, which arrived by warship in 1949.

History. The church on the shore was built in the 13th century; it fell into the sea in the 1550s and has served since 1703 as a sea-mark. The trimmed blocks of sandstone that once comprised the body of the church were filched by generations of sailors on deck-scrubbing duty, who found them just the job for gleaming planks; hence, allegedly, the naval term to 'holystone'.

St Helens was an important stopping-off point in Nelson's day; the sheltered anchorage of St Helen's Roads was usually well filled with ships taking on stores and waiting for winds of passage. The tide mill at St Helens was kept busy turning out flour (and whatever else went into ship's biscuit) to government orders; a spring in the village was the source of special water, supposed to keep fresh longer than any other, and every so often the cannon boomed out from the Point at Bembridge to warn of approaching press-gangs. In 1797 the navy mutinied at Spithead; the crisis was averted by Admiral Lord Howe being rowed from boat to boat, delivering pardons from the king. Among the winkle-

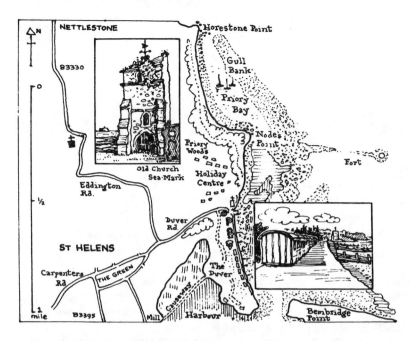

pickers watching from the shore was five-year old Sophie Dawes, the smuggler's daughter, who through colourful scandals and liaisons went on to become mistress to the Duc de Bourbon and 'Queen of Chantilly'. Her birthplace, overlooking the village green, bears a plaque.

PIERS

Between 1814 and 1910 around ninety piers were built in England and Wales, ten of them on the Island (Cowes, RYDE, Ryde Victoria, Seaview, SANDOWN, Shanklin, Ventnor, Alum Bay, TOTLAND, YARMOUTH). Today less than half survive. Most fell victim to storm and sea, though piers have also been oddly prone to catching fire. The picture is mirrored on the Island, with just four piers remaining (in capitals above).

In fact the Isle of Wight led the way with piers, Ryde Pier (1814) being the grand-daddy of them all. Still very much in use, despite having been sliced in two by a rogue ferry some years back, Ryde Pier (or piers — it is really an assemblage of structures) is also one of the longest at almost half a mile. Replacing Cowes as main point of entry, Ryde Pier did much to concentrate traffic and development of the Island along its eastern edge. Centrepiece of each new resort was its pier. Wrecked in the Great Storm of 1987, Shanklin pier could once boast a pavilion in which Pavlova danced and where artistes could fish through a dressing-room trapdoor. Sadly history does not record whether or not the great ballerina made use of this facility.

BEMBRIDGE POINT

Extensive sands at low water, can be crowded when the tide is up.

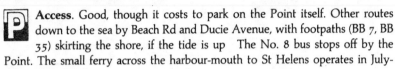

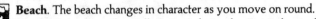

Access. Good, though it costs to park on the Point itself. Other routes down to the sea by Beach Rd and Ducie Avenue, with footpaths (BB 7, BB 35) skirting the shore, if the tide is up   The No. 8 bus stops off by the Point. The small ferry across the harbour-mouth to St Helens operates in July-Aug (10.30-5.30).

Beach. The beach changes in character as you move on round.

The Harbour, from the Toll Gate Cafe to the Point, has soft, fine sand, backed by dunes, somewhere below which lies the old sea-wall. Tucked away behind are the concrete bases of seaplane hangars from World War I. Despite the good efforts of volunteers from the local Harbour Association who organise clean-ups, the Harbour sands are often strewn with rubbish. The state of the Harbour has long been the subject of local debate.

The Point/Silver Beach: a bank of litter-gathering shingle runs along the top of the beach, below which are soft, near-level sands, which extend some ¾ mile at low-tide in the direction of the fort.

Under Tyne: Tyne Hall is one of several large houses put up in the area before Bembridge developed into its present sprawl. The beach below the trees is known as Under Tyne – or Ducie Beach, or even Garland (evoking memories of the bathing belles of the Garland Club). High-water can reach right up impeding progress along what little beach is left. Low-water rockpools, much inhabited, all the way to Forelands, with offshore bands of rock (Tyne Ledge, Ethel Ledge) parallel to the beach along to the lifeboat station. Old maps mark this rocky jumble as The Mixon – a dialect word for 'dung-heap'. Among the broken groynes midway between Bembridge and Ethel Points are the remains of a landing-place, Colonel's Hard, built for Colonel Moreton of Eastcliff, a survivor of Sir John Moore's Retreat from Corunna.

Bathing. Attractive shallow-water for children off the Point, while Under Tyne is the traditional place for bathing in Bembridge. In both spots the sheltered and relatively warm waters can attract a fair number of learner-windsurfers/jet-skiers etc., which can be a hazard. Water-quality at Bembridge (on Southern Water's list for immediate attention and permanent improvement by 1995) does not have a good record.

Safety. 'Danger!' read the signs, 'Bathing or Paddling in the Harbour or Channel is dangerous'. 'Do not bathe or play near the Channel marked by red buoys'. Beguilingly innocent of appearance, the bottle-mouth of Bembridge Harbour is hazardous both for its volume of traffic and the strength of its ebb-currents. Off the Point south-westerly breezes can sweep sailboarders and inflatables out of safety's reach more swiftly than might be imagined.

 Refreshments. Two beach cafes (Toll Gate and Silver Beach) with plenty on offer from ices and teas to locally-caught crab sandwiches . . .

Loos. Small and dismal outpost by the Pilot Boat Inn; distinctly better premises up the hill by the library. The Harold Lewis Day Centre in the High Street is the only public loo for the disabled at present in Bembridge.

Entertainment. Bembridge Festival & Regatta at the end of May is the focus for beach-events and activities, such as children's sports, greasy pole, raft-race, tug o' war, sandcastle competitions, puppet-shows . . . Not a place for bingo, deck-chairs or amusement arcades, Bembridge retains a certain debonair veneer (David Niven grew up here – Jeremy Irons was raised in St Helens, though), kept up by summer 'yachties'.

Sport. Classy local sailing-club, famous especially for the attractive little Bembridge Redwings that race off the Point. Fishing-trips (874040) from 2-hour mackerel sorties to 6-hour deep-sea runs from the harbour – with timings for departure and return dependent on the tide.

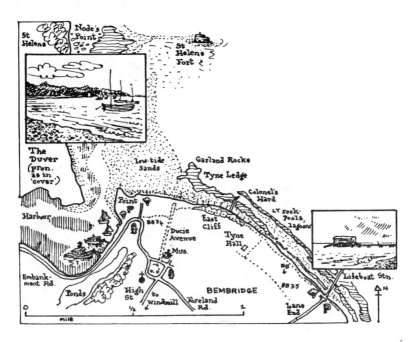

Visits. Bembridge Maritime Museum (March-Oct, 872223. 873125) is a must. Beer still fizzy from HMS *Velox*, sunk by mine in 1915; golf-balls from the *Highland Brigade*, torpedoed off St Catherine's in 1918. It is the personal items which catch the eye among the grapeshot, cannon-balls and pieces-of-eight, salvaged from the surrounding sea. When it comes to knowledge of local waters, few could be better qualified than local diver, lifeboatman and historian, Martin Woodward, whose fascinating collection, covers topics from wrecks to lifeboats, piers to lighthouses. Among the tales of local heroism detailed in the museum, one stands out above all others – that of Ethel Langton, a kind of local Grace Darling, who in 1926 alone on St Helens Fort, without food, coal or telephone-link, kept the light going through desperate storms for 3 days and 3 nights, while her parents were stranded ashore, unable to row back with supplies.

 Walks. The Walk to the Fort is a local tradition of almost 30 years. On a pre-arranged evening in July or August, when the tide is right, up to 400 people splash out seawards on the annual trek from Ducie Beach to the leaning fort of St Helens – and back again, one hopes.

 Natural History. Lots for marine-biologists in the area as well as for the amateur naturalist, from winter-visiting birds to summer flora on the dunes of the Point. The shrubbery round the car-park is Sea Buckthorn, while nearer the road grow spikes of Fragrant Evening-primrose.

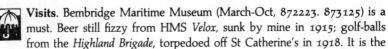 **History**. The town of Brading is, as it looks from Culver, a seaside-town cut off from the sea. Brading Haven, described in 1841 as a 'large and ugly puddle', was once a major inlet, which stopped just short of making Bembridge a separate island. In stages the land was reclaimed, chiefly by the building of the Embankment in the late 1870s. In 1882 the first train chuffed confidently over the marshes to the newly completed Spithead Hotel. But the venture was never established on a firm enough footing. Bembridge Harbour brought ruin to more than one MP. Jabez Balfour ended up in jail, protesting his innocence, when the Liberator Group crashed in 1892; a fortune had been shelled out on 750 acres of boggy land. The reverberations continue to this day, as developers, planners, engineers and residents argue on about the future of Bembridge Harbour. Multi-million pound schemes for new homes and marinas have repeatedly surfaced, but local interests seem best served by the members of Bembridge and St Helens Harbour Association, keen to preserve the natural environment and to maintain the harbour as a safe arena for family boating.

BEMBRIDGE
FORELAND

A fairly narrow rim of sand above infamous ledges much prized by marine biologists.

Access. Easy at Lane End, steeper at Foreland. Parking (at a price in summer) at Lane End and at Foreland Field (off Egerton Road). Step straight down from the sea-wall at Lane End; at Foreland, rough track down from the coastal path (BB 10) or steps by the Crab & Lobster. *Buses*: no. 8.

Beach. Line of shingle (which traps a certain amount of litter and weed) sloping down to sandy patches with pebbles, above low-tide ledges of rock. High-tide leaves only a limited stony strip (5 yds, if that) around Lane End. Main sandy areas below the new sea-wall at Foreland (Crab & Lobster) and on into Howgate Bay. In theory the pay telescope at Lane End enables you to look N to Nettlestone Point (3 miles off) and out along the line of Spithead Forts (St Helens, No Man's Land, Horse Sand, Spit Bank) to Portsmouth (6-7 miles). In practice, the machine snaps shut at the critical moment. Moving clockwise from the Lifeboat Station, fishing floats mark the position of hazardous rocks – Cole Rock, Dicky Dawes (where the local smuggler sunk his barrels till the coast was clear) and Sharpass. Further out, with the Nab Tower framed in between, marker buoys warn of Bembridge Ledge and the Princessa Shoal.

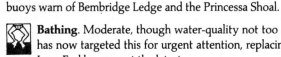

Bathing. Moderate, though water-quality not too special. Southern Water has now targeted this for urgent attention, replacing the shortfall outlet at Lane End by 1995 at the latest.

Safety. Reasonable within the areas of the beach and shallow waters. Keep well clear of the lifeboat pier. Whether this brings assurance or alarm, beaches at Lane End and Foreland are overlooked by Lifeboat and Coastguard Station, though neither is permanently manned.

Refreshments/Loos. The Crab & Lobster (872244), with food as good as its views, is the principal temptation in these parts. Beach kiosk-cafes in season at Lane End and Foreland. Huts and deckchairs from the Cabin on the Beach. Good block of loos, all year and conveniently placed, at Lane End. Temporary summer arrangement sometimes in action at Foreland.

Visits. The Lifeboat Station opens on certain afternoons (Sun, Wed, Thurs, Bank Holidays) in season for a couple of hours – unless in use. Bembridge lifeboat (estd. 1867) has taken part in many spectacular rescues, often involving boats caught out on the nearby ledges. There is no loom of land at Foreland – no cliffs for sirens to echo off – and many vessels at night or in fog have fatally misjudged their position off the eastern corner of the Island. Still just visible at low-tide (straight out from the coastguard lookout) are the remains of the *Empress Queen*, the Isle of Man paddle-steamer in use as a troopship when she ran aground in February 1916. All 110 men aboard were rescued – plus one dog and one cat – thanks to the bravery shown by the scratch crew of volunteers, who took the place of regular lifeboatmen away on service.

Walks. A nice section of coastal path (BB 10) between Foreland and Whitecliff, twisting through patches of willow ('withies'), formerly cut by fishermen for weaving into pots. The path passes in front of Bembridge School, founded by J. Howard Whitehouse M.P., Secretary to Lloyd George, educational pioneer and devotee of John Ruskin. The school's Ruskin Galleries house an important collection of pictures and papers (incl. some 5,000 letters written by Ruskin): visits by arrangement with curator.

Geology. Sea-levels were higher than at present during the warm phases between Ice Ages, as can be shown by the presence of 'raised beaches' along parts of Britain's coastline. One such ancient beach exists at Foreland, with deepening deposits of shingle and a buried cliff somewhere round Howgate, but there is little on show for the non-expert or casual visitor.

Natural History. From Ducie Avenue to Culver is an area of coastline of international significance, thanks to the diversity and wealth of marine-life there exposed. The shallow waters and intertidal pavements of the ledges are home to small creatures and a vast array of plant-life – indeed, 'the richest algal community in the country', making this a mecca for all who look into such things. What adds to the interest for scientists is the fact that the Island sits on a dividing-line between marine zones. Here East meets West, in terms of species and sub-species, with varieties of barnacle and limpet, for example, to be found at Ventnor and Whitecliff Bay, but, as yet, no further east. Whether certain species will be encouraged by global warming to spread beyond Bembridge is something now being studied. Amateur naturalists, meanwhile, can enjoy the wealth of winter bird-life usually to be found at low-tide guzzling over the ledges.

History. The Nab Tower stands 4½ miles out to sea as a lonely sentinel, visible from many parts of the Island's eastern quarter. A signpost to shipping, it welcomes vessels into the Solent, while warning of the shoal beneath. The tower was built at Shoreham in World War I with quite different purposes in mind. One of a line of towers to go in mid-Channel by way of anti-submarine defence, it might also have served as a gun-platform for bombarding the Belgian coast. Instead, peace came and the unwieldy construction was towed out to replace the ageing Nab lightship. One of the officers in charge of operations was a Captain John Reith, soon to achieve distinction in his own right as founder and first Director General of the BBC.

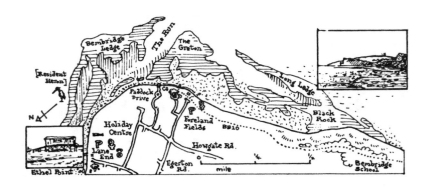

ROCKPOOLS

In low-tide pools are red seaweeds like coralweed (pink-mauve with an outer skeleton of calcium) or carragheen and dulse (supposedly edible, but tough enough to need 5 hours simmering). In among the bulkier brown weeds may be winkles of every hue, sponges, sea-squirts, tube-worms and colonies of sea-mat. Common on the rocks are beadlet anemones — out of water like blobs of jelly in red, amber or green, while the 'strawberry' variant may be spotted in Freshwater Bay. When the tide is up, these carnivores extend their 200-odd stinging tentacles to trap and devour creatures sometimes bigger than themselves. Easy to spot is the snakelocks anemone, pale brown to apple-green with non-withdrawable tentacles sometimes tipped with mauve. Shrimps and prawns are often hard to see (varying from dark shades to virtual transparency) and still harder to tell apart. Shrimps go more for sandy patches, while prawns, somewhat larger, have antennae as long as their bodies. Starfish are less common here, but some 30 species of crab live round the Island, from pea-sized porcelain crab upwards. Barnacles and limpets stick so tightly to rocks that it is often hard to believe there is life within. Barnacles cement their heads to something solid and, when submerged, wave legs to catch the passing crumb. Between grazing forays, one limpet may occupy the same spot of rock for 20 years, and few predators can shift it — apart from oyster-catchers, which know its weak spot, and dog-whelks, which sit on the shell for several days, drilling out a small hole through which to suck out the contents.

WHITECLIFF BAY

Good beach in attractive bay, worth walking down to. Plenty for water-sporters.

Access. A 10-minute walk to the surfaced track which descends steeply to the beach. The shortest routes are the footpaths (BB 15 alongside Bembridge School or BB 16 through the Holiday Centre) from Hillway, which, however, has very little space for parking. Slightly further, but more scenic, is the path down from Culver (BB 29), where you can leave the car. *Buses:* No. 8.

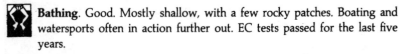

Beach. Half-mile sweep of firm sand, scattered with stones; sandier in the direction of Bembridge and more stony with seaweed towards the cliff.
Beach at shallow gradient; low-tide leaves a good expanse (suitable for cricket), though this can fill in summer and HW come right up to the stones. Privately owned, all the way down, and advertised as ' probably the Island's finest beach', which some of its neighbours might contend. *Dogs* not allowed on the beach.

Bathing. Good. Mostly shallow, with a few rocky patches. Boating and watersports often in action further out. EC tests passed for the last five years.

Safety. Beach itself quite safe, especially while watched by watersports operator (with lifeguard qualifications and equipment). Keep a safe distance from the soft crumbling chalk of Culver, round which it is easy to get trapped by the tide. No way round to Sandown.

Refreshments/Loos. Beach cafes, one at least open 7 days a week in season. Also on Culver Down, a walk up which can be rewarded with something from the Coastguard Cafe. Not to mention Culver Haven (pub & restaurant, 406107). No loos, be warned.

Sport/Hire. Whitecliff Golf & Activity Centre (May-Sept) in Hillway: golf range, putting, archery, shooting, petanque, children's pony rides ... At beach-level: plenty of different things to fall off, on hire from Waterplay (874616) — windsurfing, kayaks, paddle-boats, wave-skis, inflatable-sled rides ('The Sausage') ... Also fishing-trips and boat-trips round the bay. Beach-huts, deck-chairs, windbreaks.

Visits. Bembridge Windmill (NT, Apr-Oct, 873945) is a fine building, dating from around 1700 and little changed since last used in 1913.

Geology. Prime site (SSSI), displaying 'the most continuous Palaeogene sequence of sediments in W. Europe'. Long ago the ancient sea-beds were pushed up into waves, leaving a rapid succession of beds exposed; those by the chalk stand almost vertically on edge, while the dip levels off in the direction of the younger Bembridge Limestone. The mirror-image of Alum Bay and The Needles, the eastern tip of the Island displays within a couple of miles almost the whole range of local geology, neatly ordered like the pages of a book. Round the corner in Yaverland are the oldest exposed formations, from dinosaur times; this side of the flint-lined Upper Chalk are multi-coloured sands and clays (55 to 30 million years old), some of them rich in fossil remains from tropical lagoons. Wet-weather causes the London Clay to roll out to sea in a prominent mudflow, while ancient timbering sometimes visible west of the cafe dates back to attempts in previous centuries to mine coal from the Bracklesham Beds. The stuff extracted was brown, crumbling and 'burnt with difficulty, emitting sulphurous fumes'. From chalk debris at the foot of Culver may be found sea-urchin fossils (echinocorys), also picked up in the past on local downland and known as shepherd's crowns.

Natural History. Culver is a breeding-site for sea-birds, but don't be disappointed if it's only pigeons you see. They have a long ancestry here and the cliff is named after the Anglo-Saxon for dove.

History. Peacock Hill has resounded in summer to the banging in of tent-pegs and calling of bugles since 1905, when the London Boys' Brigade encampments first took place. The monument on Culver commemorates the Earl of Yarborough, founder of the Royal Yacht Squadron and, according to the inscription, a man 'whose benevolence, kindness of heart and many virtues endeared him to all who knew him'. Before setting off on the *Falcon*, members of his lordship's crew were obliged to sign papers which set out the merits of flogging and the cat o' nine tails.

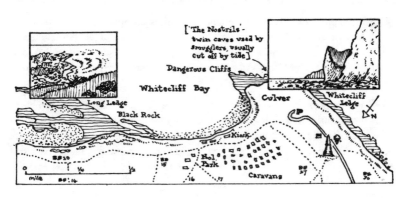

YAVERLAND

Relatively quiet and empty section of Sandown Bay.

P **Access**. Straight off the sea-wall. Well served by car-parks (pay in summer), from which it is a few steps down to the beach. If you don't like paying to park, leave the car on Culver Down and walk down (footpath SS43, with steps – when repaired – on to the beach). It's a lovely walk down, but 1½ miles to lug the picnic stuff back afterwards. *Buses*: 8 & 44.

Beach. Liable to vary a bit with the season, but usually a good long stretch of gently shelving sand below the top line of pebbles and plenty of space at low tide for cricket and football. Towards Sandown the sixteen or so groynes chop the beach up into sections, some more appetising than others, with dog-regulations in force from May to September. In the other direction, below Culver, sand gives way to chalk boulders, beyond which at low spring tide can sometimes be seen the last remains of *Harry Sharman*, the salvage tug grounded in 1970 during the operation to deal with the stricken tanker, *Pacific Glory*.

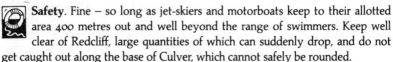

Bathing. Good. The lengthened outfall and newish treatment works have meant Yaverland passing all water-quality tests for the last few years.

Safety. Fine – so long as jet-skiers and motorboats keep to their allotted area 400 metres out and well beyond the range of swimmers. Keep well clear of Redcliff, large quantities of which can suddenly drop, and do not get caught out along the base of Culver, which cannot safely be rounded.

Refreshments/Loos. Ices and snacks on offer here – and increasingly available in the direction of Sandown – while, by the zoo, the Tiger Tavern and Cub's Den Cafe have plentiful bites. Windswept block of loos in the car-park (with disabled unit) open all year; summer only in Sandham Grounds.

Entertainment/Sport. Yaverland car-park is an occasional summer venue for circuses and funfairs – providing amusement for all but immediate neighbours. Otherwise it's down to Browns for boating and golf or Sandown for further diversions. An active sailing-club at Yaverland and the spot is favoured by windsurfers.

Visits. Nearest attraction is Sandown Zoo (403883. 405562), open Easter – Oct and welcomingly warm and dry on winter Sundays. Strong on snakes and big cats and keen to stress its commitment to conservation and research. A mile or so inland is Brading, geared up to trap the passing coachload. Places to visit include the Doll & Toy Museum (407231), Wax Museum

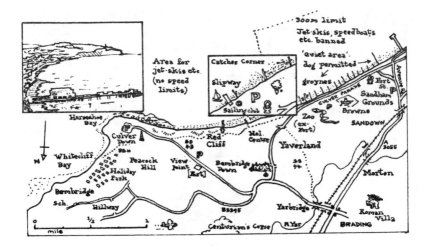

(407286), Adgestone Vineyard (402503), manor houses at Nunwell (407240), with Home Guard Museum, and Morton (406168), with gardens and vineyard, and a Roman villa (406223) with superb mosaics, perhaps not shown off to best advantage beneath the corrugated-iron exterior.

 Walks. In dry weather it's a pleasant stroll across the fields (SS 44) to Brading, where the river curls lazily round pastureland claimed from the sea. Cows permitting, there are fine walks to be had alongside the marshes, where footpaths lead ramblers over the stranded remains of the old sea-wall (B 3), through Centurion's Copse (BB 20), with its curious legends, and, ducking aircraft, up to the windmill.

Even better walks over Culver with incomparable views in all directions, ignoring the caravans. Grandstand views over the airfield and across the ledges exposed off Bembridge; beyond lies Sussex, with the Witterings some 12 miles off, Selsey Bill 14 and Chichester Cathedral, looking surprisingly large from 19-20 miles away. The view, 'seldom equalled for beauty and magnificence', was celebrated in the writings of Brading curate Legh Richmond, whose sad tales and moralising tracts were world best-sellers throughout the 19th century.

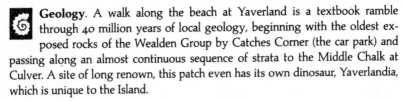 **Geology.** A walk along the beach at Yaverland is a textbook ramble through 40 million years of local geology, beginning with the oldest exposed rocks of the Wealden Group by Catches Corner (the car park) and passing along an almost continuous sequence of strata to the Middle Chalk at Culver. A site of long renown, this patch even has its own dinosaur, Yaverlandia, which is unique to the Island.

 Natural History. The rough ground of slipped cliff beyond Yaverland is another of the Island's precious coastal patches with small ponds, vegetation and burrows to harbour a rich population of species.

History. With two forts and three batteries in less than two miles (between Culver and what is now the Zoo), the anti-French scares of the 19th century led to almost panic measures, when it came to guarding Sandown beach. Redcliff Battery was the least successful of these measures, as it rapidly disappeared over the cliff. Bembridge Fort was the most awkward to build: first they had to shift the mighty Yarborough Monument from the crown of the hill, relegating it to an inferior spot half a mile away.

The dreaded shipworm ...

BORING CREATURES

As boat-owners know, there are few natural materials that cannot be bored into by some creature. Some holes are very old. Such are trace fossils — burrows made in mud now turned to stone. The sponge cliona, which uses acid to get through shell, has been drilling into oysters and limestone for millions of years. Driftwood ravaged with small holes and short tunnels is the work of the gribble, a small crustacean (1/8 in.) with a long history of gobbling up piers. It is the female that does all the work, while the male lies around in the tunnel getting under her feet. Despite name and appearance, the teredo shipworm is no worm, but a bivalve mollusc with a disproportionately long body achieved by eating up ships. Drake's Golden Hind was one of many sunk by shipworm. Infested wood may show just a pinhole on the surface. Only when split is the damage reveals — a honeycomb of twisting, lime-lined tunnels, each managing just to avoid its neighbour. Prize Bore must be the piddock, a mollusc capable of drilling into rock. The young piddock grinds out a pear-shaped burrow in which to grow fat, but from which it cannot escape. Walled up for life, the piddock spends its days reaching through its window for scraps and occasionally emitting a ghostly light from its cell, like an immured nun deep in her devotions. Piddock-shells found on the Island's north coast wash out of the clays it inhabits there.

SANDOWN

Sand, swimming and seaside-amusements galore
– though somewhat forlorn in winter.

Access. Immediate. Roads and promenades all the way along the seafront, though good weather in summer puts pressure on parking-space along the Esplanade and Culver Parade. SWBC car-parks in Fort St and Station Avenue. *Buses:* chiefly 8, 16 & 17. The railway station is half a mile back from the beach.

Beach. Good. Sandown looks east, to catch the morning sparkle on the water. In the full glare of a good afternoon the sea turns suitably blue – enough to have put imaginative Victorians in mind of Naples. Sand is plentiful; between the headlands of Culver and Dunnose, the bay boasts five miles of soft sand, washed clean by the tide. But the sea does have an unfortunate tendency to deliver more rubbish than it takes away. The beach-cleaning machine makes welcome improvements on alternate days in season, but in the rest of the year litter swept into the bay all too often stays put on the beach. Locals work hard to keep the front attractive, with Sandown Pride initiatives and projects which have netted two Beautiful Britain in Bloom Awards. But, as yet no Blue Flag. *Dogs:* seasonal restrictions with dog-prohibited area marked out centrally, beneath the Esplanade. North of this, below Culver Parade, is a dog-permitted beach, while leads, control and clean-up procedures are obligatory along the esplanades.

Bathing. Good. Sandown has done consistently well in EC water-tests (results on the notice-board at the north end of the Esplanade) and the bay is singled out for a good rating in the Marine Conservation Society's Good Beach Guide. Underfoot, things tail off a bit towards the Zoo, where the lower shore in a couple of sections has weed-strewn rock, and remnants of breakwater poking up through the sand.

Safety. Generally safe, with a good level of supervision. From May to Sept. a beach safety service operates in normal working hours, with suitably qualified and equipped local beach operators keeping watch over those in the sea. Red flags warn of unsafe bathing conditions and a First Aid Post is maintained close to the pier. Breakwaters are the main hazard: they hold sand in the bay, but often conceal a fierce (7-8ft) drop on their sheltered north side. The large slippery concrete groyne running out by Eastern Gardens, scene of more than one accident, is now well marked with warning-signs. Sandown Lifeguards, disbanded in 1958, are due to be revived in 1993.

Refreshments/Loos. Most tastes well catered for, with snack-bars, cafes and similar spilling all the way down the front. Loos are at regular intervals along the Esplanade – by Eastern Gardens, Pier Street and Ferncliff.

 Entertainment. Traditional pleasures can be indulged on the pier (dodgems, rides, fortune-telling etc.) and hungry amusement machines stand waiting in Wight City (bingo & chips) and the Arcade, as well as on the pier itself. Plenty too for energetic children, with trampolines by Eastern Gardens, and go-karts, bumper-boats and the giant slide in Sandham Grounds. The Lions Club Funtasia late in July is followed by the Regatta in mid-August (water and shore sports, inter-hotel events etc.) and Carnival events at the end of the month. The pier (originating from 1878, lengthened in 1895 – to keep up with Shanklin – and re-opened in 1990 after a major fire the previous year) houses the Pavilion theatre with traditional seaside shows and resident ghost. The rest of the town reverberates to discos and nightclubs.

 Sport. The Heights Leisure Centre (405594) in the Broadway, on the site of former barracks, has swimming-pools, sauna, squash-courts and a variety of keep-fit activities. Behind it lies the golf course (403217) in Golf Links Road, just off The Fairway. Tennis, putting and bowls are to be had at Sandham (406600), with other forms of golf along the Parade at Browns (402447). Visitors welcome at the Snooker Club in Leed St (406781).

 Hire. No shortage of things on offer along the front – deckchairs, sun-loungers, splash-cats, canoes … Huts available from half a dozen different operators, listed on the free sheet available from the Esplanade Tourist Information Centre. Boating also at Browns.

Visits. The Geology Museum (404344), free admission and open all year in library hours, is a gem of a place, displaying just a small sample of the Island's treasures. Moves are afoot to build a large new dinosaur museum at Sandham. Meanwhile, more familiar seaside rock is available for inspection at The Rock Shop (1, The High Street), which gives weekly demonstrations.

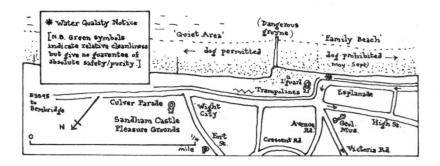

Walks. Pleasant level walks along the seafront to Shanklin (just under 2 miles from pier to ex-pier) or Yaverland and up to the monument on Culver Down. Views from Sandown usually take in a steady line of ships disappearing over the horizon; in winter-storms these scurry into the bay for shelter till winds abate. In more suitable weather, summer visitors can join afternoon cruises from Sandown (Mursell and Kemp, 403155) or take pleasure flights from the Airport (863598, 406454).

History. Sandown has gone downmarket a bit since the heady days of the late 19th century, when men of letters rubbed shoulders with monarchs along the sands. Crown Prince Frederick of Prussia brought his family to stay, including one 15 year old Wilhelm II, later Kaiser. Lewis Carroll came several times to stay and Charles Darwin worked on his *Origin of the Species* in what is now part of the Ocean Hotel. John Wilkes, the 'agitator', gave Sandown a certain notoriety in the 18th century, before which the place was little more than a barracks and fort. The granite fort now housing the Zoo is the third on the spot, or close beside; the last trace of its Stuart predecessor is a small ditch now guarding Fort Holiday caravans, while the present Sandham Fort – a pinnacled bouncy castle – is hardly what Henry VIII had in mind to defend this section of coast. None of these forts ever saw action. More recently the patch around Sandham has been the subject of several ambitious development plans, all of which have so far come to nought. The latest includes monorail, grandstand seating and underwater restaurant, somewhere below the pier.

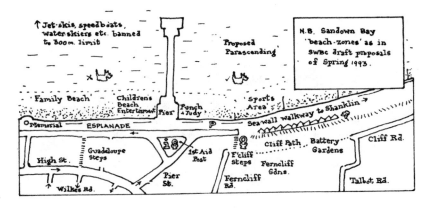

LAKE

Pleasant, sandy central part of Sandown Bay, strong on beach-huts and water sports.

Access. A few minutes walk, down or along. At first sight something of a characterless sprawl along the road from Sandown to Shanklin, Lake gives few hints of the presence of a fine beach below the cliff or of the best way down to it. Easiest may be the level walk along the sea wall from Sandown or Shanklin. The direct route is down the steps (94) from Cliff Rd, reached by Talbot and Ranelagh Roads off Lake Hill. Another path zigzags down the cliff at Littlestairs, towards Shanklin; it's just 3 mins down to the sea from the cliff-top car park (SWBC) by Winchester House, just after Skew Bridge, where the road crosses the railway. *Buses:* 8, 16, 17 & 44 ('The Big Dipper'). *Trains:* Lake Station close to beach, midway between cliff access points.

Beach. Long, but rather narrow. Soft sand, gentle waves and shallow water make this a good spot for small children (especially so with the presence of loos and absence of traffic). Beach sandy and at a gentle gradient all the way along, but it can fill up in high season – most of all at high tide, which stops just a few yards short of the sea-wall, if that. *Dogs:* seasonal restrictions in force, though not entirely clear where they apply. 100m either side of the slipway at Lake is dog-prohibited (May-Sept); beyond that to Sandown is Esplanade, along which dogs must be kept on leads and cleaned up after.

Bathing/Safety. Good bathing in the various sections between the groynes (21 in all). Off Littlestairs Point there are some slippery platforms of rock in the middle of the beach, exposed at low tide. Lifebelts all the way along and emergency phone at Dunroamin, but few obvious hazards to beware of. Water quality: good.

Refreshments/Loos. Five cafe-kiosks strung out at different levels between Sandown and Shanklin, with some surprises in store along the cliff path – such as the tea garden and seafood restaurant in the grounds of the Sea Court Hotel (403759). Seasonal loos by the Esplanade Slipway and above, in Cliff Gardens, which also has a disabled unit.

Sport/Hire. Wight Water Adventure Sports (866269) at Dunroamin offer tuition and hire of equipment for sailing, windsurfing, body-boarding, kayaks, surfing, surf-skiing, canoes. Beach huts to let at several points (403587, 404648). Putting in Cliff Gardens.

Walks. Pleasant walk along the sea-wall (floodlit in summer) or at cliff-top level, where the coastal path takes in a good few ups and downs. However, the route is well punctuated with gardens (Ferncliff, Battery, Cliff ...), views and sunny seats, all enjoyed by some of the older visitors to this patch. Cliff-top views from Lake take in the sweep of Culver cliff (3 miles off) and a steady line of Channel shipping heading out past the Nab Tower and over the horizon (12-15 miles out from your position 100-150 ft up).

Geology. The unstable cliffs of Ferruginous Sand have a long history of dropping large chunks. An extensive – and expensive – cliff stabilisation programme goes on to slow erosion. Littlestairs Point is the site of a geological fault.

Natural History. Colonised by shrubs and flowers, like broom and tree lupin (which are in fact wild, but look suspiciously domestic), the orange-red cliffs are attractively splashed with yellow and green in early summer. The orange-flowered iris in damp patches at the foot of the cliff is Montbretia, while the creeping succulent found towards Sandown is Hottentot Fig, escaped from South Africa.

History. Don't try looking for the lake, there isn't one. Lake Without Water is one of the Island's Six Wonders (Needles you cannot thread, Cowes you cannot milk, Ryde where you walk, Freshwater you cannot drink, Newport you cannot bottle). The name is meant to come from the Old English 'lacu', meaning 'small stream' – which there is, just, Scotchells Brook.

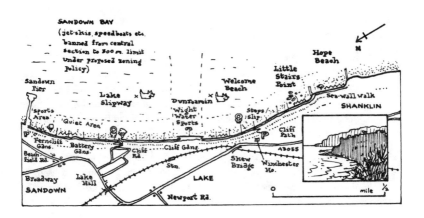

SHANKLIN
HOPE & ESPLANADE

Top tourist beaches with no shortage of sand, amusements and people.

Access. Straight off the esplanade and on to the sand. Trains and buses (8, 16, 17) will get you to Shanklin, and steep roads, the local open-top bus ('Shanklin's Pony') or the lift will get you down to the esplanade, where those with cars will find parking, if soon snapped up in summer. The lift, built in 1956, takes about 25 seconds and you spend just over a penny a second as it goes. Its predecessor was built in 1891, worked by water-balance and cost tuppence up, one penny down.

Beach. Two miles of good sand, gently shelving, with some pebbles. One rocky patch at the northern extremity, by Littlestairs Point. The section N of the esplanade, which delights in the name of Small Hope, has shelter, soft sand and some low-tide pools enjoyed by children. However, it can be very crowded in school holidays and high season. *Dogs* permitted (provided mess is removed) in this section, but prohibited (May-Sept) the rest of the way along to Shanklin Chine. The usual restrictions apply, in season, along the Esplanade. East-facing, the beach is best in the morning sun. According to the Red Guide of 1919, Shanklin 'enjoys a remarkable sunshine record, one of the highest in the kingdom. It also has an extraordinarily low death-rate'. The first of these claims at least can be substantiated: Shanklin topped the National Sunshine League for twenty of the years between 1948-1980.

Bathing. Good. Shanklin has long been favoured by bathers, though the Revd. Francis Kilvert complained at having to wear drawers. A notice in 1884 warned, 'Male Bathers are strictly forbidden to bathe from boats in front of or otherwise to intrude upon the spaces allotted for Ladies Bathing-Machines.' Water quality good.

Safety. Well run beaches, enjoying a good level of supervision (during the summer, in reasonable hours). Red flags warn of dangerous bathing conditions (undertow, breakers and swell, usually brought about by strong south-easterly winds). In season, First Aid Post (near Lift) and Beach Safety Service. Heed the signs and keep clear of breakwaters. Tide-times and water-test results posted along the Esplanade.

Refreshments. Everywhere. Three beach-cafes at the bottom of Hope Road and plenty more opportunities for stoking up as you head along the Esplanade. The Shoreside Hotel (863169), for example, has restaurant and bar, open all day every day to non-residents.

Loos. Scattered like the cafes at regular intervals along the front. Seasonal offerings on the Revetment and Esplanade (near the Lift); open all year at the Esplanade Gardens and Osborne Steps (end of Keats Green).

 Entertainment. Lots going on. The carnival in early August means attractions like dog shows and Glamorous Granny competitions, rounded off with parading bands and perhaps 30 floats in illuminated procession. Events too at beach-level (sandcastle competitions, tug o' war, swimming races) to tie in with mid-August regatta activities. Shows (local rep & musicals) at Shanklin Theatre (862739). Fairground-type attractions along the Esplanade and noisy amusement arcade alongside, housed in the former seaplane hangar brought over from Bembridge Harbour in 1921 for members of the Sunshine Concert Party (incl. Arthur Askey) to perform in. Travelling fair sometimes installed at the foot of Hope Road.

 Sport. Putting and crazy golf in the Esplanade Gardens. Bowls at Brook Road (863777). Water-sporting activities are mostly at the southern end of the esplanade and beach.

 Hire. Beach huts (863032), sun-beds and deckchairs in abundance. Sample prices for deckchairs (1992): 50p per session, 80p all day.

 Walks. Keats Green is where to saunter and promenade – with a little more confidence since the completion of rock-bolting to stabilise the cliff-top, unsettled by weather extremes since 1984. Above lies Shanklin Old Village, a wonderland of shops with twinkling trinkets, furry gorillas and extraordinary merchandise.

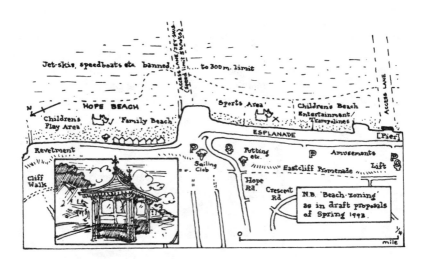

Geology. Head along the sea-wall in the direction of Lake and, just behind the beach-huts at Small Hope, you may find yourself side-stepping a nasty-looking puddle of rusty brown sludge with an oily sheen, oozing out from the base of the cliff. This is the chalybeate spring, the liquid gold on which Shanklin's early fortune was based. First hailed by Charles II's doctor, the iron-rich waters of Shanklin were deemed health-giving and curative of many ills – including overwork and a poor complexion. Never a match for Bath or Chelten-ham, Shanklin nevertheless grew as a spa town, dispensing ferruginous showers and sea-water baths, hot or cold – amazingly, people paid a shilling a go for the latter.

Natural History. Jellyfish are commonly washed up in Sandown Bay and elsewhere, especially in June/July, when their remains in the sunshine are distinctly short-lived. Jellyfish are 95% water. Most likely to be seen are the Common or Moon Jellyfish (up to about 10 ins across and with distinctive markings in the form of four mauve crescents). Compass Jellyfish are usually bigger (perhaps 18 ins across, with 24 brown streaks radiating out), while Rhizos-toma Octopus (really a jellyfish) may be larger still (2ft across, with what looks like a fairly massive apparatus of dangling tubes).

History. Something of a Costa del Sol of its day, Sandown Bay developed almost from nowhere in the course of the 19th century. The population of Shanklin went from about 250 in the 1840s to some 4,500 by the turn of the century. Not that such growth was over-hasty or done on the cheap. Shanklin always had the edge over its neighbours in terms of sedateness and taste. A French visitor at the turn of the century found much to admire in Shanklin and including the sun ('so English') and the striking absence of pros-titutes. Certainly the cast-list of notable residents in Shanklin's heyday reads like something from Agatha Christie – Lady Isobel Atherley, Mr White Popham, General Viney, Silas Kemp, Poppy Colenutt, Lady Hatherton, Mr Spartali, Mr Scaramanga, the Bastianis ... There was always something a bit cosmopolitan and classy about Shanklin. King Alphonso of Spain stayed here, at the Royal Spa Hotel, as did the German royal family. Indeed, the Kaiser's youngest son left the hotel in 1914 only hours before the declaration of war. The hotel was destroyed in World War II. All that remains is the flagstaff (by the site of the pier) and an empty space, debated over for 40 years, but still just used as a car-park.

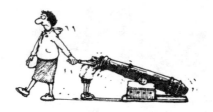

SHANKLIN
APPLEY

Pleasant sandy beach, but noisy if jet-skis are in business.

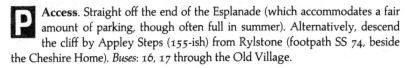

Access. Straight off the end of the Esplanade (which accommodates a fair amount of parking, though often full in summer). Alternatively, descend the cliff by Appley Steps (155-ish) from Rylstone (footpath SS 74, beside the Cheshire Home). *Buses*: 16, 17 through the Old Village.

Beach. Sand, deckchairs and boating activities. High tide can leave little beach exposed, but at low water Appley has a good expanse of firm, flattish sand with space to set up stumps or kick a ball. From the Chine to Appley Steps is dog-permitted, subject to the usual conditions. North of the Chine is a popular patch that can soon fill up in summer. This section of beach, as along in Shanklin and in other resorts, is run by licensed longshoremen, who pay a hefty sum to the council for rights upon the beach. The chairs are theirs and you pay to use them.

Completed in 1891, the pier was wrecked in the Great Storm of 1987 and finally removed in 1993.

Bathing/Safety. Good – the same comments apply as to the previous section on Shanklin (Hope Esplanade). Keep well clear of boating activities and beware also of leaving valuables unattended along the front.

Refreshments/Loos. No shortage of feeding-posts, from the Esplanade cafes to the tea-rooms at Rylstone and The Chine. Most scenic is the pub on the beach, Fisherman's Cottage (863882), serving meals as well as pints. A fair sprinkling of loos – in season at Osborne Steps, Chine Bluff and Rylstone Gardens; all year at Tower Cottage Gardens (by the Chine) and the Town Hall. The last three have disabled units.

Entertainment. Occasional band performances in Rylstone Gardens (as posted through the season), but nothing to compare with former times – like the open-air dances of the 60s or the pre-war evening concerts which drew crowds of 2-3,000. The Friends of the Old Village Association work hard to provide free midweek entertainments for summer evenings. Watch out too for special events at Big Meade, such as fairs and Town Criers' Conventions.

Sport/Hire. A great deal at beach-level: huts (863958), splash-cats, motor-boat trips, as well as jet-ski hire (0831-253730) and other rides (ski-biscuits and banana boat). Away from the beach, crazy golf in Rylstone Gardens and riding at Luccombe Riding School (862074), Cowleaze Hill.

Visits. For years the I.W. Natural History & Archaeological Society put on a display each August ('Local Look') at Brook; now that has transferred to a more extended summer arrangement in the Swiss Chalet at Rylstone. Alongside is The Chine (866432 Easter-Oct), including a fine display in the Heritage Centre. The Chine's wartime history adds to its interest. From the Chine (and from Sandown) ran the forked Pipeline Under The Ocean, carrying petrol 65 miles across the Channel to Nacqueville, near Cherbourg, to fuel the Normandy Landings. A bit of PLUTO is still in the Chine. Also commemorated are the Commandos who lost their lives in the Dieppe Raid two years before D-Day.

Walks. Attractive routes at several levels, from paths (SS 10, 11) up on to Shanklin Down (773ft) to the beach-walk round to Luccombe (low-tide needed over the ledges). In between is a fine coastal ramble (SS 2, 3) in the direction of Luccombe and the Landslip, with peeps of the sea below Dunnose. On July 25th 1588 the wind dropped and Islanders held their breath as the Spanish Armada lay becalmed off Dunnose. Everyone wondered whether the Duke of Medina Sidonia might follow the example of the French 43 years before and go for a quick landing on the Island to boost morale. Guns fired and the water churned with frantic rowing as the Spanish galleons and English vessels behind fought for position just a mile off land. Then the weather freshened and the fleets moved on up the Channel.

Geology. The headland of Dunnose is a prominent feature marking off the end of Sandown Bay. For obvious reasons the Isle of Wight was chosen as starting-point for the first mapping operations carried out by the Ordnance Survey (1793-1810) and Dunnose became one of the base points for the subsequent triangulation of all England. North of Dunnose, between Luccombe and Shanklin Chines, is Knock Cliff, with Ferruginous Sands beneath beds of Sandrock. Both bear fossils, with bivalves and brachiopods to be found on Horse and Yellow Ledges, while ancient driftwood and burrows appear from the Sandrock.

Natural History. Famous for its unusual vegetation, the Chine has just the right conditions for non-flowering plants, like mosses, ferns, horsetails and lichens. In the damp are to be found nine species of liverwort, the most primitive of all plants.

History. Standing on the beach at the beginning of the 19th century, William Cooke pronounced, 'Looking up from hence the chine presents the happiest mixture of the grand and beautiful, the awful and the pleasing.' For all its commercialisation, Shanklin has retained quiet corners and some of the charm which attracted poets such as Keats, Gerard Manley Hopkins and Longfellow, the American author of 'Hiawatha' who left some none-too-special verse for the drinking-fountain in the Old Village.

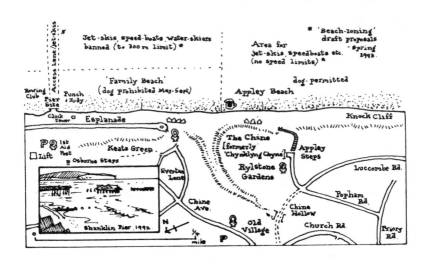

PEBBLES

In Victorian times pebble-collecting was something of a craze, and the Island is still well rated by pebblers. The hard part is knowing what to look for, as most stones look much the same.

As a cliff erodes, soft material is swept away, leaving the hardest mineral (mainly forms of silica from quartz to flint) to roll about as shingle. Flints often have markings and cavities (left by the fossil sponges round which they set) lined with small crystals of clear quartz, known locally, if optimistically, as Wight Diamonds: or Ventnor Diamonds — or wherever. Pebbles of limestone and chalk (which fizz gently under vinegar) accumulate as flattish ovals at either end of the Island. Among them may be Sandown Stars — marcasite nodules which crack open to reveal a pattern of needles radiating out (and then go rusty).

Happily the Island does not depend on its rocks alone for the pebbles along its shore. Longshore drift brings stones zigzaging up the coast from Cornwall — jasper, carnelian, translucent quartz. Catch them wet by the water's edge, where they are most easily spotted. All the quartz family share one intriguing characteristic: bang them together hard in the dark and they produce a small flash and distinctive smell, not unlike a burnt brussel-sprout. They do this underwater too — but don't ask me how any one managed to check the smell.

LUCCOMBE

Scenic, secluded cove in a dramatic setting. A good area for walks, but limited as a beach.

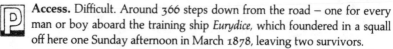

Access. Difficult. Around 366 steps down from the road – one for every man or boy aboard the training ship *Eurydice*, which foundered in a squall off here one Sunday afternoon in March 1878, leaving two survivors.

Car-parks to either side of Smugglers Haven. *Bus routes* 16, 16A, 17, 45. There are 140 steps down to Dunnose Cottage, another 226 at the last count down to the shore and twice as many back up again – especially if, unable to stop, you carry on up Nansen Hill (down which shepherd boys once whizzed on horses' skulls). The beach walk from Shanklin is pleasant, but should be done on a falling tide – it is easy to be caught out in the 350yd section between Horse and Yellow Lodges. The tide also sweeps up to the base of the cliffs in Luccombe; you wouldn't be the first to have to wade back to the steps at the foot of the chine.

Beach. Sandy patches with stones towards Shanklin, at the southern end. No amenities at beach-level to spoil its timeless wildness, but tempting tea-shops (and ices) on the way down – and up – with Dunnose Cottage at the head of the chine and Smugglers Haven and Luccombe Tea Garden a little way on in either direction.

Background. Until forced off by landslip in 1910, a small community of 5 families (with evocative names – the Buttons, the Hardys, 'Pound Hammer' Kingswell) lived in primitive cottages, with a chapel alongside, on the lower cliff edge, now home only to interesting flowers. Higher up, Luccombe Village has grown over an ancient landslip system, recently reactivated, to the concern of local home-owners. The forbidding cliffs of tiered sandstone, layered like cake with fillings of clay, drop fossil wood and cycad cones from 106 million years ago on to the beach below. Smuggling thrived in this dark, hidden corner; the caves still visible in the chine and the ledges running out to sea (Johnny New Rocks) have housed many a barrel of fortifying substances.

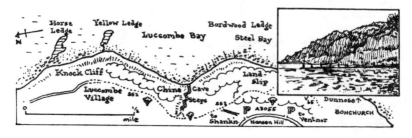

BONCHURCH

Small patches of beach in attractive location, still Victorian.

Access. *Monks Bay*: a short way round on the sea-wall from Horseshoe Bay; can also be reached by footpath (V 67-9) below the Old Church or (V 65) down from the Landslip (with free parking just before or just beyond Smugglers' Haven). *Buses*: 16, 17.

Horseshoe Bay: Shore Road, opposite the Pond, leads right down to the bay, with a large car-park (SWBC, pay in summer) just before you hit the bottom. The new sea-wall from here to Ventnor makes a level ¾ mile walk around three stony bays.

Beach. Variable, with little to show at high-water. Sheltered from the prevailing winds, Bonchurch is nevertheless one corner of the Island round which the sea can sweep in lively style – the choppy waters of the tidal race off Dunnose can be spotted from the cliff-top. It is also a spot with an unstable geological foundation. The result is a long swathe of concrete, below which are boulders, rockpools and some sandy patches, especially at low-tide. From *Horseshoe Bay* to Ventnor the sea-wall is complete, with not much in the way of beach alongside. Increasingly rocky towards Ventnor, with Cat Rock exposed at low-water in Wheelers Bay. Originally Hudson Bay, this last inlet takes its name from the Wheeler brothers of Blackgang. Their father, caught smuggling, was sentenced to serve 5 years on a man-o'-war; he jumped ship on the west coast of S. America and spent 2 years walking across the continent to the east coast, where almost the first person he bumped into was an officer from the ship he had deserted.

Monks Bay: transformed by the completion in 1992 of a million-pound coastal defence scheme. A whole new beach has been made, protected by an offshore breakwater consisting of large parts of Sweden (24,000 tons of rock) dumped by barge.

Bathing/Safety. Best in the sandy section between groynes. One foul-water outfall in Horseshoe Bay, due to go out of commission by 1995. No water-tests. Monks Bay can accumulate seaweed. Reasonably safe in good weather – though this is the spot where the *Underley* was wrecked in 1871. The steward was the only casualty, drowned, it was said, trying to save his pet canary.

Refreshments/Loos. Bay House Cafe (with seafood specialities) and Horseshoe Bay Hotel provide for all needs. Loos. Horseshoe Bay (seasonal), a small bog with literary associations: Dickens showered here, or at least in the waterfall behind and long before the present premises appeared.

Visits. Small pottery in enviable position. Also small is the Old Church, steeped in atmosphere (though, at 48ft 6ins long by 12ft wide, it is a third longer than the old church at St Lawrence). Charles I came here to attend the funeral of a cavalier killed in his service.

Walks. The walk through the Landslip (V 65) is one of the Island's classic rambles, with something for everyone. The result of major slips in 1810 and 1818, the place had a fascination for visitors in the last century. With its lush vegetation and cool shade, the romantic scenery of the Landslip was in perfect accord with Victorian sensibilities. An SSSI rich in wildlife (foxes, woodpeckers, butterflies . . .), the area is dotted with things of interest for children: the Devil's Chimney, the Wishing Seat, shelters and lookout points, as well as the stepped walkways newly completed by the Countryside Management Service. Occasional glimpses out over 5 miles of Sandown Bay to Culver, with Bembridge Foreland peeping out behind.

Natural History. The cliffs support a colourful carpeting of seaside flora — red valerian, rock sea-spurrey, sea-kale (like cabbage with white flowers) and hoary stock, colonising the base (one spot where the flower's famous aroma can be sampled without fear of plummeting over a cliff). Out to sea may occasionally be seen gannets, presumably from Alderney, the nearest of the British Isles' 17 gannetries. Two-thirds of the world's population of gannets inhabit the British coastline.

History. The Battle of Bonchurch (1545) was a relatively small affair, all part of the day's events on July 19th, when the French made four simultaneous but confused landings on the Island and left empty-handed. The raid on Bonchurch (aiming perhaps for Appuldurcombe, where Henry VIII had been not long before) led to 'a hot skirmish' around the site of what is now the

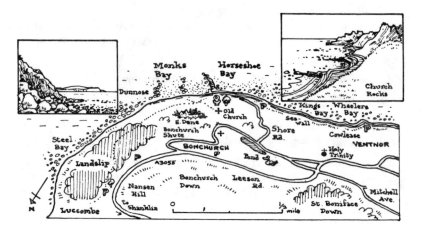

Hillside Hotel and tactical withdrawal, as local forces swept down from above. In later years Bonchurch stone was quarried for Portsmouth dockyards; but it was the 19th century that saw the place really come into its own, with a list of residents and visitors that reads like a Who's Who to English Literature. Dickens wrote six chapters of *David Copperfield* here; Macaulay worked on his *History of England*. Swinburne, born and buried here, grew up at East Dene. H. de Vere Stacpoole wrote *The Blue Lagoon* — and presented the pond. Thackeray holidayed here and Keats, Carlyle, Tennyson and Longfellow all visited. The fame of Bonchurch spread and spread; visitors came by the thousand. Pleasant spot it may have been, but one cannot help wondering if contemporary descriptions erred on the side of exaggeration: 'the most beautiful thing on the sea-coast this side of Genoa' (Dr Arnold). 'Certainly one of the fairest spots the average traveller is likely to see in the course of a lifetime' (Ward Lock Guide). Or Elizabeth Sewell: ' sometimes it has seemed to me that heaven itself can scarcely be more beautiful . . . ' which, as a 1920 guidebook drily adds, rather lowers one's anticipations of the future.

VENTNOR
Family resort with plenty for small children.

 Access. Immediate access from the Esplanade, down steps to the beach. Car-parks (SWBC) above the Esplanade, at either end, and room to park along it in winter. *Buses*: 2A, 16, 17.

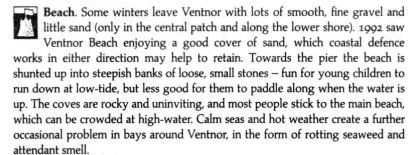 **Beach**. Some winters leave Ventnor with lots of smooth, fine gravel and little sand (only in the central patch and along the lower shore). 1992 saw Ventnor Beach enjoying a good cover of sand, which coastal defence works in either direction may help to retain. Towards the pier the beach is shunted up into steepish banks of loose, small stones – fun for young children to run down at low-tide, but less good for them to paddle along when the water is up. The coves are rocky and uninviting, and most people stick to the main beach, which can be crowded at high-water. Calm seas and hot weather create a further occasional problem in bays around Ventnor, in the form of rotting seaweed and attendant smell.

Dogs: check the signs to see exactly where seasonal restrictions apply. Dog-prohibited beach from Linnington to Waters Edge; dog-permitted between Linnington Groyne and Swales Groyne. Usual restrictions along the Esplanade.

The Pier: Ventnor's third and last pier, fire damaged in 1985, was finally removed in 1993 to make way for a new breakwater/jetty. Councils and townsfolk have for years been locked in sometimes acrimonious debate over Ventnor's future; schemes have included a harbour, marina, continental fast-ferry terminal, waterside village, funicular railway, cable-car, trams ... The same arguments raged about Ventnor for much of the last century; a harbour was begun in 1863, but was beaten by the elements within four years.

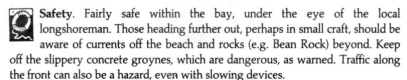 **Bathing**. Mostly good. Waves can wash quite strongly on to the beach, which shelves fairly steeply towards the pier. Water-quality not good, with EC tests failed over six years. The outlets at Flowers Brook and Collins Point are clearly in need of attention; this has been promised by Southern Water, unveiling multi-million pound plans to tackle Ventnor's problems by 1995. Perhaps summer water-quality explains why many locals choose Boxing Day for their annual dip!

Safety. Fairly safe within the bay, under the eye of the local longshoreman. Those heading further out, perhaps in small craft, should be aware of currents off the beach and rocks (e.g. Bean Rock) beyond. Keep off the slippery concrete groynes, which are dangerous, as warned. Traffic along the front can also be a hazard, even with slowing devices.

Refreshments. Plenty of cafe-kiosks and sea-front establishments dispensing drinks and ices, few of them better placed scenically than the Spyglass Inn (855338), with real ales, live lobsters and seafaring memorabilia. If that's not your cup of tea, try the Ventnor & Bonchurch Temperance Society Drinking Fountain at the other end of the Esplanade.

 Loos. Chiefly on the Eastern Esplanade (between the Cascade and the Paddling Pool). Above sea-level, premises in Albert Square, Marlborough Road and Bath Road (seasonal); climb right up to the top of the hill and you'll find the one disabled unit (Newport Road).

 Entertainment. The carnival, going now for more than a century, takes place in mid-August. More dressing up in June with the more recently instituted Smuggling Pageant, involving costume battles between smugglers and militia. Events as advertised in the Winter Gardens (855111). Amusement Arcade (The Gaiety) in central position along the Esplanade. East of the pier is a good range of things for children – boating lake, crazy golf, go-karts ... not forgetting the old favourite, the Isle of Wight Paddling Pool.

 Sport/Hire. Deckchairs, windbreaks, boats, beach-huts (for fairly lean and agile folk) ... Bowls at Mitchell Avenue (854235).

 Visits. The loss of the railway was a serious blow to Ventnor, leaving the town out on a limb, over the hill and all at sea ... Always something of a place apart, Ventnor has struggled to survive recession. But, if question marks hang over present and future, Ventnor has a glorious past to hang on to. The Local History Society is very active and both the Heritage Centre (855407) and the Longshoreman's Museum (853176) are splendid local enterprises – with modest admission rates – celebrating former times. The Longshoreman's Museum on the Esplanade, run by the Blake family (like much else over the years on Ventnor shore), has a small shop to cater for all tourist needs (fossilized crocodile droppings included) and a fine display of photographs, artefacts and tableaux.

 Walks. Good walks along the seafront to Bonchurch and, over Western ·Cliffs to Steephill, with Woody Point peeping out beyond. Alternatively, conquer the Island's highest point, St Boniface (787 ft) by the direct route up the south face (footpath V1), setting off from the former railway yard, now Industrial Estate, off Mitchell Avenue. The easier way is by car up Down Lane. St Boniface is one hill that Jack and Jill could have gone up to fetch a pail of water: two-thirds of the way up the steepest side, above St Boniface School (but now lost in the scrubby cover of evergreen oak) is a well, imbued with special powers. Traditionally 'dressed' on St Boniface's Day (June 5th), the Wishing Well would grant to any who reached the spot without looking back three wishes formed while drinking its water.

 Geology. Official surveys show that over the last ten years 15% of Ventnor's houses have suffered some slippage, activated by water-drainage in an unstable arrangement of rocks (solid sandstone on slippery Gault clay). There is nothing new about this. Ventnor is along the 7-mile stretch of ancient landslip from Bonchurch to Blackgang, which is reckoned among the most extensive and spectacular landslips in Europe. It is not all bad news: Ventnor is a sun-trap and a special climate is enjoyed by the Undercliff, a strip of terrace, up to half a mile wide, south-facing and sheltered by the 100-250ft backdrop of inner cliff. In Victorian times, Ventnor was deemed 'the healthiest spot in the kingdom' – and local builders never looked back.

Natural History. Good for cormorants, allegedly only seen here flying from left to right. Members of the pelican family, cormorants have non-waterproof feathers, which they must hold out to dry – hence the preaching position on rocks and nickname Isle of Wight Parson. Cormorants, with white cheek and thigh patches on adults in summer, are not easy to tell apart from the slightly smaller and thinner shags, which sport crests in courtship plumage. The green cormorant or shag came close to extinction here in the last century; 'doomed victim of the collector', it was hunted for hats.

History. In 1838 Ventnor was no more than a hamlet of fishermen's cottages, housing 350. By 1870 the population was up to 5,000. Tidy minds objected to the hotch-potch mature of the town's expansion, 'without plan, without order, without method'. But Ventnor's disorderly growth soon attracted a remarkable line-up of famous, or soon-to-be-famous, visitors. Churchill loved Ventnor: holidays with his nurse at her sister's home in Dudley Road featured among the young Winston's earliest childhood memories. Karl Marx came twice for his chest. Gandhi visited in 1890 and the Emperor Haile Selassie stayed in what is now the Beach Hotel. Turgenev had to move out of his lodgings, because his landlady objected to his friend's smoking. Musicians, in particular, seemed

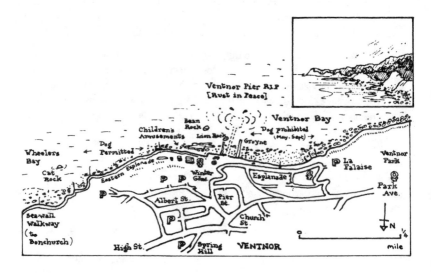

drawn to Ventnor: Jenny Lind, the Swedish nightingale, came briefly to roost. The Elgars honeymooned in what is now the Bermuda Guest House. Edwin Lemare, composer of 'Moonlight and Roses', lived here and Ralph Butler (who wrote the lyrics to 'Nellie the Elephant' and 'Run, Rabbit, Run') had a flat in Albert Street.

Most books attribute Ventnor's rise to one man, Sir James Clark, royal doctor and author of a book on health-care and weather. 'The Sanative Influence of Climate . . . With an Account of the Best Places of Resort for Invalids in England' turned Ventnor almost overnight from fishing-cove into 'The Madeira of England'. What the guidebooks do not say is that Sir James was not one whose judgement was above question. He it was who assured Victoria, just days before Albert's death, that all was well and there was no need to seek a second opinion. Equally tragic was his mishandling of the sad affair of Lady Flora Hastings, a young lady at court who fell victim to malicious gossip, whispering of pregnancy. Instead she died of a tumour. Perhaps medicine and the unfortunate Sir James were just not meant for one another. Having begun as a lawyer, Clark changed professions and joined the navy as ship's doctor. His ship promptly sank. Surviving this, he joined another – which also sank.

VENTNOR STEEPHILL

Small cove, secluded and self-contained, with basic amenities in a picturesque setting.

Access. Steep hill, brisk walk. Park in the Botanic Garden (*buses: 16, 16B, 17, 31*) and sooner or later, in the direction of the sea, you will hit the path and steps that drop down into the cove. Or, park (again, at a price) at La Falaise, on the western extremity of the Esplanade, and follow the paths through Ventnor Park and down to Steephill (about ¾ mile). No access by road.

Beach. Well sheltered and a sun-trap for much of the day. The beach, privately owned but run for public use, is well provided with facilities, yet manages to retain some of its original character and charm as a small fishing cove. However, it can fill up in season and high water leaves little space on the beach. Low tide reveals a sandy area scattered with boulders, gently shelving between rocky platforms, bolstered by large blocks of alien pink Mendip stone newly brought in for coastal defence. Well carpeted at the time of writing, Steephill can lose much of its covering sand to winter storms, which deliver instead unwelcome supplies of litter and oil.

Bathing/Safety. Safe bathing best in the central sandy area, keeping well clear of the rocks. Unstable chalk cliffs and sea-barriers of large boulder could be of hazard to the adventurous-minded of any age. Water-quality dubious and likely to remain so till the completion (due in 1995) of a major scheme to replace old shortfall outlets at Steephill and Flowers Brook.

Refreshments. Cafe at beach-level specialising in local seafood, freshly caught, in addition to usual range of ices, teas and whatever. Licensed premises (The Garden Tavern, 853254) up the hill in the Botanic Garden, also with picnic area, cafe/restaurant etc.

Loos. Small affairs in season at Steephill Cove and Ventnor Park (near the road); those at the Botanic Garden (open all year and equipped with disabled unit) are distinctly preferable.

Entertainment. Plenty along the coast in Ventnor. Steephill itself is one spot without 'amusements' or much in the way of commercialisation. Children's play area in the Botanic Garden, which is also the venue in May for the one-day Crab Fayre.

Sport. Ventnor Cricket Club's ground at Steephill is the Island's Oval. 9-hole golf course off Steephill Down Road (853326), as well as putting in Ventnor Park and Flowers Brook. Angling – good for night-time bass.

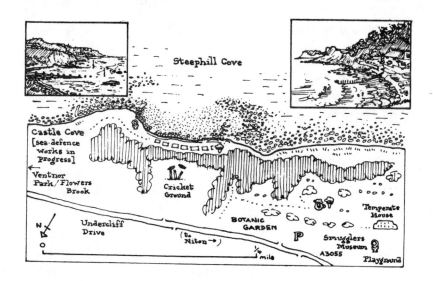

Steephill Cove

Castle Cove
[sea-defence
works in
progress]

← Ventnor
Park / Flowers
Brook

Cricket
Ground

N

Undercliff
Drive

(to
Niton →)

BOTANIC
GARDEN

P

Temperate
House

Smugglers
Museum

A3055

Playground

¼ mile

Hire. Deckchairs, windbreaks, huts, rowing-boats, canoes and even holiday accommodation all for hire from the Beach Man (at 'Genevra'). Modest and rather thin people can pay to make use of the ancient changing-cabins, which are probably the last vestiges of bathing-machine in use on the Island.

Visits. Free admission to the Botanic Garden (855397), but pay to park. Open all year, the place is given Grade I status in the Good Gardens Guide, which puts it 'amongst the best gardens in the world in terms of design and content'. Gardening enthusiasts and those without umbrellas will not begrudge the small charge to enter the Temperate House. Even more sheltered is the Museum of Smuggling History (Easter-Sept, 853677), located in the cellars of the former National Hospital for Diseases of the Chest, which closed in 1964. 'Favourite resort of invalids and honeymoon-couples' is the old jibe about the Island in general and Ventnor in particular. Whether Ventnor's hills did more to kill or cure the patients is open to question, but the fresh air and out-door jobs were deemed most beneficial.

Walks. Ventnor Park, in the grounds of the former Steephill Castle, is a fine wide public space for children to charge about in, with winding paths and stepping-stones for the traditional fall into Flowers Brook.

Geology. Peer over the edge of the Western Cliffs and, on a clear day, you may just see parts of Somerset ... somewhere below your feet. 30,000 tons of rock from Frome have been deposited at the base of the weak chalk cliffs in a bid to hold back erosion.

73

Natural History. If looking down into Castle Cove in early summer, admire the cliff flora, including Hoary Stock, fragrant, pink-mauve and looking like a garden escapee, but in fact the reverse: this is the original wild stock from which domesticated species have been cultivated.

History. Steephill Castle, where the Empress of Austria and family spent their summer holidays in 1874, was built as a Gothic fantasy in the 1830s and pulled down in the 1960s to make way for bungalows. The place seems to have had something of a jinx on it: the head mason was killed by a falling block of stone during construction, which the onset of blindness prevented its owner from ever seeing complete. In 1893 his descendant and heir to the estate, the 20-year-old Cecil Hambrough, lost his life in a shooting incident in Scotland, which became something of a cause *célèbre*.

FISHING

Wight lays claim to some of the best fishing in Britain for bass, cod, sting-ray, sole and tope. British records have been notched up locally for catches from shore rockling to thresher shark. 'Not like it used to be' is a common grumble among anglers, though one borne out by statistics. The mackerel shoals have gone, but around the Island at least 37 species are regularly caught – most regularly pout.

The creeks and mud of the Island's north coast tend to provide mullet, eel and flounder, with bass in summer, cod in winter. Sandy stretches between Ryde and Shanklin are best for flatfish – plaice, sole, flounder – with pollack and garfish round rocks and piers. Along the gravelly shore of the S.W. coast, skate and rays are to be had after an onshore blow with bass, pollack and conger best after dark. The Solent entrance by Ft Victoria is a prime spot, in season, for close-in bass and cod (up to 29 lbs). Conger eels like the Island coastline for its many wrecks and rocky holes in which to lurk. Recorded up to 15 ft, with razor-sharp teeth and the rare ability to go as well in reverse as forwards, the conger is a formidable catch.

ST LAWRENCE

A fine coastal walk. No beach facilities, but several Places to Visit.

 Access. In most cases a fairly rugged walk from whichever direction.
Orchard Bay (or 'Orchard's Bay or 'St Lawrence Cove'): park in the Botanic Garden and head right to find the coastal path, which soon leads off down to the bay.

(*Sir Richard's Cove*, where Sir Richard Worsley of Appuldurcombe kept a battery of captured French cannon parked on the cliff: rocky and inaccessible.)

Woody Bay (or 'Hoody Bay'): carry on along the coastal path for another ¾ mile. Alternatively, approach from Wolverton Road (just a few spaces to leave a car), below which endless footpaths meet up round the Sugar Loaf in a tangle. Choose path V 98 down to the Bay. The last bit on to the shore is sometimes eroded, overgrown and hard to negotiate, but has recently acquired new steps.

Binnel Bay: park at Old Park (well-signed), from where it's a 10-minute walk to the shore. Head past the hotel, through woods and down steps through a tunnel of greenery to the sea.

Buses: 16B & 17 pass along the Undercliff and 31 diverts to Old Park.

 Beach.
Orchard Bay: private beach allowing public use, below highwater-mark, on strict conditions – no radios, tape-recorders, dogs, topless sun bathing, ball-games, frisbees, boating, canoeing, sunbeds, fishing, tents, stone-throwing, fires, barbecues, trespassing ... All of which make this a very civilised spot for anyone generous-minded enough not to be consumed with sheer envy at the sight of house and bay. Beach of gritty sand and small stones, running down to larger rocks at low tide.

Pelham Cove: occasional sandy patches among fine gravel, leading down to bouldery section with low-tide pools inhabited by small crabs, anemones and shrimps. Fossil-rich rocks at either end.

Woody Bay: mostly pebbles and fine gravel.

Binnel Bay: a little sand at low-tide, but pretty elusive. Rocky shoreline with rough boulders of Upper Greensand worn into attractive pebbles. Mud, weed and rocks in the direction of Puckaster.

Bathing/Safety. Orchard Bay is your best bet; elsewhere, the rocky shoreline does not lend itself to bathing. Foulwater sea-outfall at St Lawrence/Willow Wood (between Binnel and Woody Bay).

Visits. The Rare Breeds and Waterfowl Park (Spring-Oct, 852582). Llamas, deer, knee-high horses and cattle like hearthrugs ... unusual breeds now occupy 30 acres of Undercliff farmland, causing walkers on the coastal path to blink and look twice. Not much further along at Old Park is the Tropical Bird Park (852583), with Isle of Wight Glass (open almost all year, 853526) close alongside. A small charge admits visitors to see (Mon-Fri) the hand-crafting of fine glass.

Walks. For two miles, from Ventnor to the Sugar Loaf, the coastal path rollercoasters along the chalk cliffs, disappearing through tunnels of twisted hawthorn to emerge at vantage-points with changing views of shipwreck rocks and smugglers' coves. At one time there were ten coastguard stations between Ventnor and The Needles, but never enough to combat local ingenuity. At Woody Bay the eroding coastal path now diverts round the back of the coastguard cottages, enabling you perhaps to avoid the local spook, the Lady in Black. Equally dramatic is the grandstand view from the path over the inner cliff, rising to 463ft at High Hat above St Lawrence and reached by St Rhadegund's Steps (from Seven Sisters Rd). The seat at the top commands fine views over the slipped ledge of the Undercliff to the far horizon – 26 miles on a clear day.

Geology. The shoreline is scattered with blocks of Upper Greensand, rich in shellfish fossils and the burrowing traces of worms that bored through the sand a hundred million years ago. Many such blocks have slipped from above, travelling perhaps half a mile from escarpment to beach.

Natural History. Growing at Binnel – and many other parts of the Island coastline – is a tough, feathery shrub with red branches ending in spikes of small, pinkish-white flowers. It is tamarisk, introduced from the Mediterranean in Tudor times and commonly found by the sea. Good as a windbreak, tamarisk has roots that bind unstable dunes and supple stems that can be used like willow as 'withies' for weaving into lobster-pots.

History. The Undercliff can count a good few grandees among its former inhabitants. The look-out towers and belvederes of their fine houses stick out from the greenery of St Lawrence like the heads of dowager duchesses in boxes at the theatre. Earl Jellicoe lived at St Lawrence Hall, now burnt down – only its gate-pillars remain. Lisle Combe – the one with the twisted chimneys – belonged first to Capt Pelham, son of Lord Yarborough, and later to the poet Alfred Noyes. The Orchard, towards Niton, was built for Sir Willoughby Gordon (friend and adviser to the Duke of Wellington in Spain) and visited by Turner, who painted the scene. But the name most commonly associated with St Lawrence is that of Herr Spindler. A wealthy industrialist, grown rich on the making of Indigo Blue, William Spindler came to Ventnor from Germany in 1873, broken down by overwork. Recovering his health, the over-active Spindler set about organising Ventnor. In 1877 he produced a wonderfully opinionated little

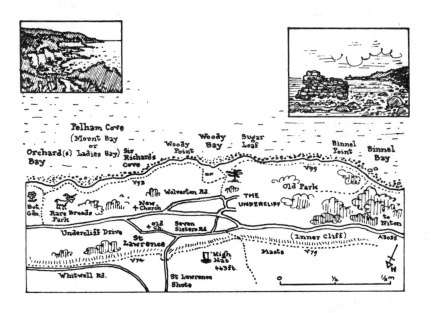

book, *A Few Remarks about Ventnor*, which can hardly have endeared him to the natives. 'Grasping Grumblers,' 'Meddle and Muddle' and 'General Laziness' are just some of its headings. Determined to show the way, Spindler acquired Old Park and embarked upon a massive scheme to build a harbour and, in effect, whole new town along the coastal strip. But Ventnor had the last laugh. The harbour, only a very small part of which was completed before his death, was built on clay. Several large chunks of masonry, known as Spindler's Folly, still rise from the sea at Binnel. But not all Spindler's efforts were in vain; a great tree-man, Spindler is the person to thank for much of the woodland about St Lawrence.

NITON

Not much accessible beach left thanks to erosion.

 Access. Whichever way you choose, it's a longish walk down a steepish slope. St Catherine's Rd, off Undercliff Drive (*bus* services 16, 17), has some space for roadside parking at either end (the Buddle car-park is for patrons only). Don't try driving on down Castlehaven Lane or the private road to the lighthouse, but follow these on foot for half a mile to *Reeth Bay* or the National Trust property round Knowles Farm, which brings you down in another 300 yds to *Watershoot Bay*. Dock Lane, opposite the Buddle, is a short cut to *Reeth Bay* saving the zig but leaving the zag of Castlehaven Lane. To general dismay, the old way down Puckaster Lane to the cove was closed in 1990, as, for the umpteenth time, a large area of cliff gave way to erosion. The nearest path down is (NT 50) by The Orchard, along Undercliff Drive (no parking – leave the car in Niton). Jostled by stingers and bramble, the path is best not tackled in bikini or shorts. At sea-level, *Puckaster* can be reached from Castlehaven only at low-tide, and then with difficulty over loose rock and seaweed.

 Beach. The southernmost part of the Island has a losing battle with the sea. *Puckaster*, where Charles II blew ashore in 1675 'after enduring a great and dangerous storm at sea', once had fishermen's huts and an intriguing Bath House, the ground floor of which filled with bathing-water at high tide. Now it is a jumble of rock, with some sandy patches in the centre and attractive low-tide rockpools.

Reeth Bay, also referred to as Castlehaven or Castle Cove, once had a sandy beach with bathing-machines and a short-lived (1851-75), three-storied hotel on a headland now swept away. Reeth or Wraith Bay takes its name in grisly fashion from the bodies of shipwrecked mariners swept into the bay on the backward swirl of the west-going Channel stream.

Watershoot Bay, round the corner to the west, was once a smugglers' cove, with boathouse and slip. Watershoot is now just a rocky inlet, liable to collect marine debris and litter. Shark Rock shows just above water at the entrance to the small bay, while Shag Rock is the large boulder on the corner.

 Bathing/Safety. Possible in Puckaster at high-tide, taking care to avoid submerged rocks, and at Castlehaven in the cleared channel, avoiding boats. Moderately safe within the inner haven, sheltered by rocks; very dangerous beyond, where strong currents sweep round. No information on water-quality, but no mains outfalls in the vicinity.

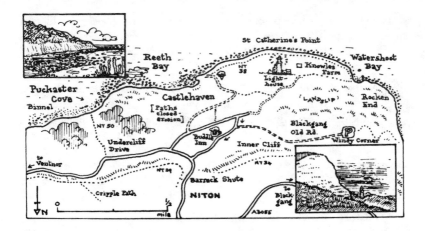

 Refreshments/Loos. Snacks and ices at The Oasis, small outpost by the caravan-site at Castlehaven. Tempting food and drink at The Buddle Inn (children welcome). The nearest loos are in Church St, Niton – a long way to go.

Visits. St Catherine's Lighthouse (730284), due for automation in the next 5 years, is open free to the public, in smallish numbers, on Mon-Sat afternoons, Easter-Sept, weather permitting (not in fog) and subject to operational commitments. Two-thirds of its original height when opened in 1840, the lighthouse is still tall enough to give anyone queasy about heights a giddy turn. Worth climbing, though, not just for the views and keeper's talk. The light shows 25 miles in good weather, rather less than its 1900s predecessor, which claimed the most powerful beam in the world. Tragically, all three keepers were killed in a single air-raid in 1943.

Walks. Niton is good walking territory at different levels in several directions. The land cliff can be scaled by the Cripple Path (NT 117, opp. Little Orchard) by those bold enough to brave the ledges of crumbling chert. In the last century a local girl, Kerenhappuch Newnham, survived being blown over this cliff, saved by the ballooning breadth of her dress. The old coach-road to Blackgang leads to an area of ancient landslip (NT property), which is a wonderland of ridges and hollows, carpeted in spring with cowslips and violets. Grassy mounds look out over the sinister waters of St Catherine's Race, where the headland protrudes into a fast-moving tidal stream. Close to the surface just three miles out, a bow-shaped ridge runs parallel to the shore; between the two lies St Catherine's Deep, a channel of turbulent water up to 300 ft deep, in which ships are known to have sunk without trace.

 Geology. The old road continued to Blackgang till July 26th 1928, when a quarter of a million tons of rock collapsed in spectacular style, burying 150 yds of road in tumbled cliff. Just one of many landslips over thousands of years on this spot, where porous rock sits uneasily on the slippery shoulders of impermeable gault. Back-tilted slabs poke through the terraced landslip, while the shoreline is jumbled with blocks of Upper Greensand, rich in fossils one hundred million years old.

Natural History. From March to May dedicated folk huddle at St Catherine's in the two or three hours after dawn to peer through binoculars at small dots mostly going from right to left; the spring passage of migrant seabirds (divers, skuas, terns, auks ...) is a treat for the serious birdwatcher. Salt winds and sea-spray make it possible for only certain plants to survive on cliff-tops. One such is Rock Samphire, to be seen on the cliff between Castlehaven and the lighthouse. Strong on iodine and good against scurvy, the plant takes its name from 'herbe de Saint Pierre' (the patron saint of sailors).

History. Knowles Farm is where Marconi carried out radio experiments, using a mast from the Royal Yacht Britannia. Niton is still famous for its radio-masts, used for communications with Channel shipping on marine bands. In the 19th century, Niton was known chiefly for its waters. The chalybeate spring attracted eminent visitors, including Queen Victoria as a girl, to stay at the nearby Sandrock Hotel (now burnt down). The waters were much prized by an army doctor at Parkhurst, who found them 'eminently useful in chronic cases of debility'. The water contained 'an unusual proportion of alum and iron, held in solution by sulphuric acid'.

SEA VIEWS

Visibility is limited by two factors, clarity of the atmosphere and curvature of the Earth. To work out how far the horizon is out to sea, there is a generally accepted formula: multiply your height in feet above sea-level by 1.5 and find the square root (surprisingly simple with a calculator). The answer is in miles.

Thus, a reasonably tall person at the water's edge can see only about 3 miles out to sea — and even then the horizon may be obscured by sea-spray. Fifty feet up, as at Hanover Point, and the horizon is 8-9 miles off; a hundred feet up, as at Atherfield, and the distance is 12-13 miles. From the Tennyson Monument (482 ft) it is about 27 miles to the horizon; from the highest point on the Island, 787 ft up on St. Boniface, you should in theory see just over 34 miles out to sea, should the weather ever permit it.

BACK O'THE WIGHT
ST CATHERINE'S TO FRESHWATER

On the map it's a pretty straight line of coast that runs from St Catherine's to Freshwater, one planed smooth by weather and sea. From the viewpoints of Rocken End or Blackgang, the coastline changes – clearly divided by headlands of resistant sandstone at Atherfield and Brook into the separate bays of Chale, Brighstone, Brook and Compton, with several lesser kinks and wobbles in between.

Except at spring high tides there is beach most of the way along, making it possible in theory at low tide to walk the ten miles from Rocken End to Compton. In practice few would manage it for the time and effort required to trudge through the gravel of the first few miles. Ways down from cliff-top to sea are few and far between: most people cluster round the access-points and think of these (Whale Chine, Chilton etc.) as separate beaches. For the purposes of this guide, such spots have been grouped together into main bays and headed accordingly.

Access is difficult, sand limited and unreliable, facilities almost non-existent and safety at a premium all the way to The Needles. Ask any local, though, and, likely as not, he or she will point to this section if called upon to nominate a favourite beach. The raw, primeval scenery and sheer vigour of the elements along this exposed coastline more than make up for its lack of deckchairs and kiosks.

CHALE BAY
ROCKEN END TO ATHERFIELD
Wild and wonderful, nature in the raw.

Access. Difficult, sometimes very. Free parking at *Whale Chine*, the Isle of Wight's answer to the Grand Canyon. Here the descent to the shore is an alarming drop over the edge, with 146-odd steps to negotiate at various angles and the last twenty feet in a state of constant erosion. The nearest alternative in either direction (Rocken End/Blackgang or Shepherd's Chine/Atherfield) means plodding almost two miles through soft gravel, tide permitting, to reach this middle part of Chale Bay. Path sometimes closed in winter.

Rocken End (commonly referred to as Blackgang): small free car-park at the end of the dangerously narrow Blackgang Old Road (off Buddle Lane, Niton). A good 10-15 minutes to the beach down a slippery path (wet or dry) over unstable landslip, including at one point a 20ft rope-assisted slither, though each year the route changes. *Buses: 16, 17.*

Beach. Gravelly shingle at a shallow gradient – smooth small stones, graded by size, with occasional sandy patches along the lower shore and towards Atherfield Point. Here and by Whale Chine, high spring tides can reach to the base of the cliffs. 'Probably this south-western coast of Wight is the longest stretch of unspoiled and colossal landscape in the south-west of England'. Apart from the actual position of the cliffs, which a century ago were 400 yds further out, nothing much has changed here in the forty years since John Bet-

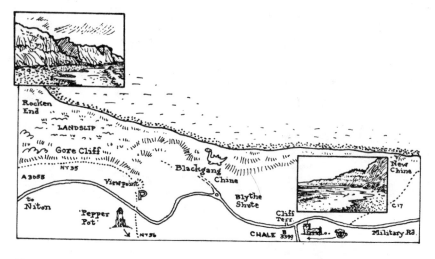

jeman wrote the above words. There is something elemental and timeless about this coastline; for most of its length, not a car, not a house nor any sign of twentieth-century life can be seen from beach-level – apart from litter. There are no facilities here, just bare cliffs that can build up a wall of heat in the afternoon sun. It is a place for sunbathers, generally starkers. Rocken End to Blackgang is 'the nudie beach' – but it's not obligatory. Chale, wrote Albin in 1831, is the 'rudest and most savage part of Vectis shore'.

 Bathing. Considerable caution required. Often a tempting blue, the sea here is fresh and invigorating, not to say downright cold. It can also be distinctly dangerous, with a powerful undertow (even when calm on the surface) and a mischievous tendency to deliver every so often, without warning, the most almighty wave, much bigger than the rest. The sea-floor shelves steeply off Whale Chine, leaving bathers soon out of their depth.

Safety. (See above). Few provisions should trouble arise; emergency phone at the top of Whale Chine. Be very wary, too, of the cliffs here, which are prone to sudden collapse.

Refreshments/Loos. One intrepid ice-cream van, out in all seasons and weathers at Whale Chine; another usually to be found in the view-point car-park above Blackgang. Midway between lies the Wight Mouse/Clarendon Hotel, open all day, all year (apart from Sundays, 3-7pm) and one place you can be sure of finding food and taking children. No loos from Ventnor to Brook.

Entertainment. Perched 400 ft up and dropping fast, *Blackgang Chine* (730330, open Easter-Oct, floodlit at night May-Sept) is a fantasy theme park, much enjoyed by children. Others may prefer the separate heritage exhibitions (Timber and Maritime Worlds), which contain interesting and authentic local material. Here too may be found the skeleton of the whale – said to be the largest found round the British Isles – which washed up at the Needles in

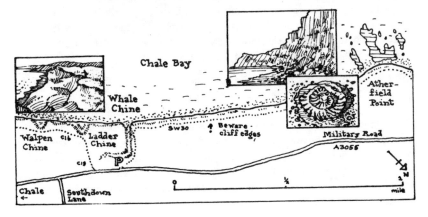

1842 (the year Blackgang first opened as a public attraction). Extraordinary, not least because the skeleton seems to have measured 75ft in the 1970s and grown 12ft in the years since. 'This awful chasm . . . dreadful to behold . . . inspiring the mind with horror . . .' So wrote visitors to the Chine two centuries ago, well before the sea cut back the cliff to its present position – 250 yds have gone since 1940. The Chine itself is fast disappearing, and with it has gone the dark path or 'black gang' down the gloomy ravine, which probably gave the place its name. Forget the geology, the real cause of the erosion is Henry VIII, who closed down St Catherine's Oratory ('The Pepper Pot'), leaving its priest to put a curse on Chale: 'The earth shall crumble and crumble away / And crumble on till Judgement Day.'

 Sport. The beach at Whale Chine is a favourite haunt of night anglers, with lanterns twinkling on the surf. Chale Bay, especially after gales, provides a grand variety of fish – painted rays, dogfish, mackerel, bream.

 Walks. Times have changed, but not the difficulties of access, since 1854, when Gideon Mantell wrote of Atherfield, 'This path is too precipitous and inconvenient to be attempted without risk by ladies or invalids.' Ways down the cliff are still hazardous. Between Niton and Brighstone the coastal path offers splendid views to all brave enough to look, but in places it runs perilously close to the edge of the crumbling cliffs. Around Whale Chine the path is held up by daisies and striped sea-bindweed. Back towards Blackgang, the path skirts the vestiges of chines which once led down to fishermen's huts on the shore. Ladder Chine, negotiable fifty years ago, now ends in a 150ft drop. Iron Age middens (pits filled with kitchen refuse – animal bones, limpet and winkle shells) discovered along these cliffs tell something of its early inhabitants; no doubt archaeologists of the future will be grateful to those who continue the tradition by dumping cookers and waste in the windblown bowl of Walpen Chine. Above Blackgang viewpoint the path leads through sea-campion (rare on the Island) and over Gore Cliff to Niton. Windy Corner, scene of the 1928 landslide, has now been reclaimed by nature; the inner cliff rings to the noisy alarm of birds on ledges sometimes visited by peregrines. Those cagey about heights and cliff-edges may prefer the equally fine walk over St Catherine's Hill and down to the Hoy Monument, the curious ball-topped pillar erected to commemorate the visit to Britain in 1814 of Tsar Alexander I. Still more curious is the later addition of a memorial tablet to those who fell in the Crimean War.

 Geology. A spot much favoured by fossil-hunters over the years, not least for the many large ammonites yielded by the Lower Greensand around Whale Chine. Towards Atherfield, fossils abound in the Lower Gryphaea Beds along the beach and in the concretions of 'Crackers' rock near the Point. Lobsters, oysters, bivalves and brachiopods have been fixed in the sands for some 110 million years. Red, brown, grey, but rarely green, the iron-rich bands of Lower Greensand go rusty in air. Common along the beach are the phosphatic nodules and irregular masses of iron pyrites washed out of the Ferruginous Sands.

Natural History. At the beginning of this century lookouts took up positions on the cliff-tops in May for the arrival of the mackerel shoals. Indeed till 1758 Whale Chine was known as 'Mackerel Rail'. But in that year a 63ft whale washed up at the chine, which was promptly re-named. The whale itself had quite a history: having been captured, dead, by the 64-gun man-o-war, *Alcide*, it was in the course of being towed up the Channel when lost off The Needles. Over the years several whales have landed up on the Island, including one in 1888 which had collided with a ferry in the Solent. It was displayed in a tent at Seaview, but admission prices tumbled when the smell got too strong.

History. A quarter of a million wrecks are scattered round the coastline of Britain, more than any other country in the world. Four thousand known wrecks are charted in the area of the Solent Approaches – and that figure ignores vessels salvaged and those sunk without trace. A great deal of shipping has come to grief in Chale Bay, worst of the Island coastline's many black spots. Time and again vessels have misjudged their position to be sucked into the bay by tidal indraught and driven helpless on to the rock by prevailing winds. At least 60 ships were lost this way between 1746 and 1808 – fourteen grounded in one memorable night. One of the earliest known wrecks was the *Sainte Marie de Bayonne* in 1313. By most accounts it was the loss of the ship's cargo of wine that most hurt the ecclesiastical authorities for whom it was destined; the chief local beneficiary was obliged by the Pope to build the chapel-cum-lighthouse on St Catherine's by way of penance. After the Roman pharos at Dover, the Pepper Pot is Britain's oldest lighthouse. Its replacement, the 'Salt Cellar' (or 'Mustard Pot'), was begun alongside in 1785, but never completed. It took the *Clarendon* disaster of 1836 to galvanise people into building a proper lighthouse on the southern-most point of the Island. Broken to pieces on the beach in less than five minutes, to the ghastly accompaniment of passengers' screams and imploding ship's piano, the *Clarendon* left a deep scar in local memory. After the *Sirenia* disaster of 1888, a new lifeboat was set up on the cliff at Atherfield, near where boats now seemingly dangle in mid-air. To reach the sea, the boat slithered down a 240ft runway of sleepers. With seven Cottons in the crew, the Atherfield lifeboat saved 157 lives in the course of its 39 launches (1890-1915). In the end steam power, telecommunication and improved navigational aids brought a sudden drop in the number of vessels foundering at Chale. Shipwrecks gave way to houses being lost in the bay. Five properties fell in the most recent major landslip at Blackgang (1978). A walk along Cliff Terrace (off Blythe Shute) reveals the problem that remains.

BRIGHSTONE BAY
ATHERFIELD TO SUDMOOR

A long stretch of attractive empty coastline, with
sandy beaches at low tide worth walking to.

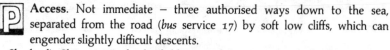

Access. Not immediate – three authorised ways down to the sea,
separated from the road (*bus* service 17) by soft low cliffs, which can
engender slightly difficult descents.

Shepherd's Chine: just E of Atherfield Bay Holiday Camp, space for a few cars on
the verge. Footpath (SW 25) heads down the Chine for ¼ mile and ends in
wooden steps – or not, according to the ravages of the sea. (The track down
Cowleaze Chine is not a public right of way.)

Grange Chine: where the road comes down from Brighstone, with some space
for cars just off the Military Road, opposite Barney's Road House. Footpath (BS
57) leads you through the camping-site and on to the beach in less than 5 mins
(300 yds).

Chilton Chine: small free car-park just after I.W. Pearl. Footpath (BS 72) brings
you shortly down to the beach – how shortly depends on the state of the steps.

Beach. Brighstone Bay looks south-west to catch the summer sun and
winter winds, and the sea here sparkles. Due west is Dorset, with Anvil
Point and Durlston Head often visible across roughly 25 miles of English
Channel. Brighstone Bay changes from steep shelving shingle, at its southern
end, to more gently angled sands, with low-tide ledges in between. High water
leaves very little beach exposed at a number of points between Ship Ledge and
Brook. It also leaves rather a lot of seaborne litter. Off Atherfield Point are three
notorious ledges (The Bench, The Mexon and Typet), exposed at low water to
reveal slippery rock, interesting pools and occasional bits of wrecked shipping.
The same goes for Ship Ledge, midway between Barnes High and Grange Chine.
The beach at *Atherfield*, towards the Point, has accumulated a good deal of
soft sand lately, in which is planted the up-ended brick remains of the former
coastguard lookout's air-raid shelter. That the structure is still intact after its
nosedive over the cliff should give satisfaction to its wartime builders. This end
of the bay is an occasional haunt of solitary anglers or lone nudists or sometimes
even both in one, which is living dangerously. For the next mile in the direction
of Brighstone, the beach is mostly gravel, scalloped into small bays and shunted
up into steep banks in three tiers, with larger stones on top, descending to
sandy patches below. Beyond Barnes High (the yellow sandstone highpoint in
the cliffs), the beach evens out to gritty sand with stones and continues thus
to *Chilton*. Here the beach has a 25 yd wide strip of sand at the top, which
soon gives way to the slippery platform of purple and mottled mudstone. As

elsewhere, the chine at Chilton gets tarred plastic and ocean-going litter blown up it in winter. More interesting are the chunks of concrete dating back to the 30s, when the aristocratic builder of the large house above was busy constructing a hangar and hoisting-gear for his seaplane.

Bathing. Reasonable, best at HW. Sea hard to reach at LW across slithery rock. The shingly sections of Atherfield, like Chale, drop steeply away, with a powerful undertow – dangerous conditions, especially for children and non-swimmers. In the rest of Brighstone Bay, where offshore rocks hold in place a good base of sand, bathing is generally safe and good. The water should be clean, despite its cloudy, brown appearance, caused by fine sand in lively waves. However, Brighstone fared poorly in NRA tests for 1992.

Safety. As ever, beware of cliff-falls. Not that you could help being pressed close to the cliffs if caught out by the tide, which can come right up between Chilton and Brook and around Ship Ledge. Being cut off temporarily may prevent you returning the way you wish, at the time you wish, but should not be dangerous, if you stay your ground.

Refreshments/Loos. Brighstone Tea Gardens (740229) is your nearest cuppa. Or Isle of Wight Pearl, open all year, seven days a week. Nothing at beach-level, but Barney's Roadhouse (740844) is well placed by the Military Road. No loos nearer than Brighstone – off Main Road, with disabled unit.

Visits. A little way inland is Yafford Mill & Farm Park (740610), which combines rural history with things for children. Handy for anyone feeling under-dressed on the beach, Isle of Wight Pearl (740352) is free to enter and a place to which coachloads string along.

Walks. An attractive walk over the coastal path – but no connecting-routes between beach and cliff for 2 miles from Cowleaze to Grange. Instead, midway there is a nicely positioned seat at Barnes High, in memory of WJBR and EVR, who would have wished you, like them, to enjoy a perfect sunset from this spot. Barnes Chine itself has long since disappeared. 200 years ago it was described as 'a vast chasm in the earth ... (which) inspires the mind with horror ... The entrance has the appearance of leading to some subterraneous passage which furnishes a retreat for a nest of robbers'. Certainly the coast round Brighstone was far from accessible before the creation of the Military Road, built in the 1860s as a defensive connecting-route and opened to the public only in the 1930s. With the sea eating fast into parts beyond Brook, and a new section of bypass ruled out on conservation grounds, the Military Road seems set for a short life.

Geology. The red sandstone cliffs of Brighstone have yielded a great many bits of dinosaur. Most commonly found are remains of iguanodon – a 25-30 ft herbivore, which probably moved and munched in herds – and its smaller cousin, the fast-moving Hypsilophodon. The latter was established as a separate species by the Revd William Fox, who spent 20 years collecting fossils on Brighstone's beaches. He failed to progress beyond curate (according to the vicar's wife, 'It was the bones first and the parish next . . . '), but several dinosaurs now bear his name. When Fox died in 1881, his collection of some thousand-odd specimens was snapped up by the Natural History Museum. Dinosaur bones do not come two a penny, but you cannot miss the lignite/fossil wood of the same vintage scattered on the shore. There are dark bands in the cliff (esp. E of Grange Chine), which contain carbonised plant debris and bits of fish and crocodile originally caught up in a mud-bar of the floodplain. Between Cowleaze and Shepherd's Chine the rock changes to the paper-thin shales of the Vectis Formation – fine layers of grey mud from coastal lagoons, interspersed with limestone paving-slabs packed with shells of the mussel-like bivalve, filosina. Half a mile on, things change again, as the fossil-rich Perna Bed emerges from the sand by Atherfield Point. Trapped in the rock are the shells and hard parts of creatures that lived on the shallow sea bed 3 million years ago. Easy to spot are the pitted bulges of the coral Holocystis, looking like ancient golfballs.

Natural History. Idyllic in high summer, the cliff-top scenery is far from hospitable in winter winds. The coastal area of Atherfield is a treeless plateau with hedges blasted and bent. Thrift or sea-pink, salt-tolerant, flowering April-Oct and retaining its colour even when dried, is one of the few plants hardy enough to survive these conditions. Other wildlife, seeks refuge in the chines, whose twisting, landward ends provide shelter and undergrowth. Carved out by streams in late Glacial times (when the sea was some 80ft below its present level and the coast a mile further off), the chines are specialised habitats with flora and fauna that make unusual neighbours. Come March-April, the chines spring into life, sunshine bringing out of hibernation the woolly, black, red-headed caterpillars of the Granville Fritillary, ready to munch on Ribwort Plantain. Not many weeks later this coastline sees other butterflies arrive from warmer parts – Red Admirals from the continent, Clouded Yellows from the Mediterranean, Painted Ladies all the way from Africa. At sea-level, as on the land above, wildlife survives the elements by cowering in crevices. From windows in Farringford, Tennyson could see ships smashed to pieces on the ledges of the SW coast, yet marvel at the powers of its colonising small creatures,

'Frail, but of force to withstand,
Year upon year, the shock
Of cataract seas that snap
The three-decker's oaken spine
Athwart the ledges of rock,
Here on the Breton strand . . . '

History. Ship Ledge, Dutchman's Hole ... the place-names recall the many wrecks claimed by this coastline. Housed where caravans now sit at the foot of Grange Chine, Brighstone lifeboat saved 433 souls in its time, 1860-1916. Three incidents stand out above the rest – the wreck of the *Cedarine* (1862) with her cargo of ex-convicts, who celebrated their dramatic landfall by drinking the village dry; the *Sirenia* tragedy (1888), in conditions which claimed the lives of three local lifeboatmen, and the *Eider* grounding (1892), which took 41 trips to bring ashore 379 people and the bullion she carried. As well as lifeboatmen, Brighstone is famous for bishops (three) and smugglers without number. The fine rectory, in whose garden Bishop Ken wrote 'Awake My Soul', is where William Wilberforce, the slave abolitionist, died. His youngest son, Bishop Samuel, was the original 'Soapy Sam'. Brighstone is rich in legends and ghost tales, mostly fabricated by smugglers keen to keep nosy persons safely indoors on certain dark nights. Most moving of all is the story of the Thimble cairn, which used to stand on the downs, marking the spot where a young girl sat and sewed for her wedding, one eye watchful on the horizon, as she pined for her sailor-love. She sewed till her death, but he never came back.

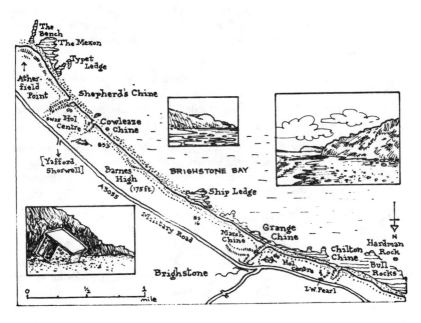

BROOK

Moderately sandy beach in an attractive bay, with much to interest geologist and naturalist.

Access. Just a minute or two from the NT car-park to the beach down the old lifeboat launch-path, an important access for boats, being the only one left between Freshwater and Niton. Alternatively, the other side of the chine, behind the old lifeboat house is usually to be found a flight of steps in various states of repair. *Buses:* 17, 1B.

Beach. Brook looks west to Purbeck, with St Alban's Head looming 26 miles off. Gently shelving, the bay is sandy, stony or rocky, according to the state of the tide, which at high water leaves little beach exposed. Eastwards, it is easy to get cut off – with no escape up the cliff – around Sudmoor, where the tide comes in fast over the flat ledges. A National Trust property, where dogs are permitted, Brook is not spared litter problems: voluntary groups doing spring-cleans have no difficulty filling 80 or more sacks with tarred plastic and other rubbish blown up the chine each winter.

Bathing/Safety. Best at highish tide and well away from fishing gear. NRA testing in 1992 showed the water quality here to be poor; discharges into the stream to be tackled by 1995. Fine sand swirling over the ledges also makes the water very brown. Bathing moderate – best in the central part of the bay. Poor at low tide. Reasonably safe in normal conditions. Emergency phone at the top of the chine.

Refreshments/Loos. Good quality ice-cream van in the car-park during summer. Across the road is Hanover House (740553), 'the Island's oldest Restaurant and Tea Gardens'. Mobile loos wheeled down below the car-park each summer; just mind you're not inside when it gets towed away.

Visits. Chessell Pottery (78248), just off the B3399: watch porcelain shaped – all hand-made, with no two items ever quite the same. Garden-enthusiasts should watch out for the occasional open days at Mottistone Manor, and Owl Cottage in the same village.

Walks. The coastal path in summer from Chilton to Brook is a fine cliff-top ramble, bright with butterflies and carpeted with Greek legends. The abundant white flower Yarrow (Achillea millefolium) was used, according to Homer, by Achilles to treat his soldiers' wounds. Centaury, the attractive pink flower growing on the slumped cliff, takes its name from the centaur Chiron, who was healed by this plant. The path loses sight of the modern road with all its traffic, and looks across instead to the thatched roofs and small steepled churches of Brook and Mottistone, set against the Downs. Ramblers can explore Brook along ancient by-ways and forgotten coach-roads through Hulverstone, Downton and Dunsbury.

Geology. Dinosaur territory with rolled bones, trackways and footprints to be found in the exposed deposits (115-113 million years old) of the Wealden floodplain. In 1977 nearly thirty dinosaur footprints were discovered on the shore west of Chilton Chine.

Natural History. From below it's a mess; from above, one can soon understand why aptly-named Roughland Cliff is of special importance to scientists and conservationists. The broken ground of slipped cliff is the preserve of nature, providing homes in its cracks and terraces, ponds and undergrowth, to a rich variety of cherished species — orchids and reedmace, newts and toads, dragonfly and woodpecker . . . in short, a thriving community, well served by erosion.

History. Brook Hill House juts out like the bridge of a ship, as its architect intended. Heavily modelled on Dartmouth Naval College, the house was begun in 1914 for Sir Charles Seely, and was later home for ten years to the writer and broadcaster, J.B. Priestley. In the next generation, General Jack Seely, Ist Lord Mottistone, served as coxswain in the lifeboat at Brook, which in its time (1860-1937) saved 263 lives. The coast round Brook is hemmed in by ledges and individual rocks, some of which show at low water (Stag Rocks off Sudmoor, Hardman Rock towards Chilton). Launching the lifeboat was a feat in itself, requiring furious rowing and sharp navigation through the gap in the rocks.

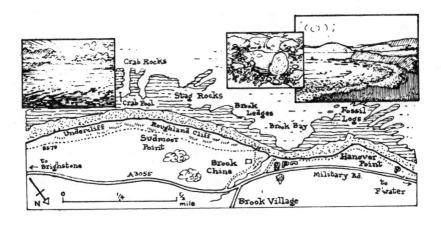

COMPTON

A mile-long sweep of sand, with stones, much favoured by the locals.

Access. A fair descent. *Shippards Chine* (also known as *Compton Grange* but commonly referred to as *Hanover Point*): steps and slope to beach below.

This car-park can fill up in summer, but beware of overflowing on the verge and obstructing the road – cars have been towed away.

Compton Chine: in field at farm entrance, 7-8 min. walk down to beach. Cross road (at dangerous corner) into field, turn left along old coastguard track to stile, descend new steps and path over slipping undercliff to sea – this can be a scramble. The old route straight down Compton Chine is no longer possible.

Afton Down: large lay-by. 10-15 min. walk through field rich in flora (and thistles), cross footbridge over Chine stream to join up with route above. Keep clear of cliff edge. *Buses:* 1B, 17.

Beach. Plenty of sand, some a funny colour. Dogs banned, May-Sept, Hanover Point to Freshwater Cliffs. A good length of beach, but the tide can come right up in places, leaving no width at all. Eastwards, you can round Hanover Point into Brook Bay; westwards, progress is not possible much beyond the beginning of the chalk and any attempt may lead to being cut off by the tide. This far end of the beach is where occasional nudies sport. Upper sections of beach sandy with stones, leading down to smooth ledges in parallel lines exposed at low tide. From Shippards Chine to Hanover Point much of the foreshore consists of slippery rock and soft, eroded mudstone. Deserted for much of the year, Compton attracts quite large numbers in summer as the main sandy beach on the S.W. side of the Island, open to the ocean and supposedly free from inshore pollution. By the same token, however, Compton is exposed to the prevailing sou'westerly winds and is on the receiving end of whatever the Channel delivers – even coconuts from Barbados 3,600 miles away.

Compton beach provides an attractive view west to Freshwater Bay, backed by Tennyson Down. Beyond lies Purbeck in Dorset (St. Aldhelm's Head), 20 off. The other way is Hanover Point, a band of hard sandstone on which many vessels have come to grief. In November 1871 the schooner *Hephzibah* and the barque *Cassandra* hit the rocks within three days of each other. However, the sea-mark, known as the Thimble, was put up in the last century not for shipping, but to indicate the limit of fire for novice gunners banging away from Fort Redoubt at Freshwater (now the tea-rooms). The small wreck exposed by the tide is the tug *Carbon*, which made a spirited bid for freedom in 1947, when it broke from its tow to the scrapyard. It is now happily beached and home to conger eels.

Bathing. Generally safe but beware of undertow strong enough to drag a swimmer out to sea. Shallow a long way out, though not always pleasant underfoot with weedy rock and occasional obstructions. Long breakers make Compton a favourite with surfers, esp. in spring and autumn. Low tide leaves good puddles and pools for small children. The unwelcome-looking boxed outfall at Shippards Chine is a natural stream and not a raw sewage outlet. Water quality good: EC tests passed with high ratings over 5 years, apart from occasional brown foam caused by algal blooms in summer.

 Safety. Good, away from cliff edges. Large waves can cause trouble to non-swimmers, but the main hazard is with cliff-falls, especially between Shippards Chine and Hanover Point, where large sections of loose sandy rock can drop without warning. The rest of Compton Bay is eroding at an equally alarming rate, but much of the cliff has already slumped, leaving a more gradual incline. Beach warden in summer.

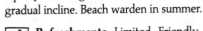

 Refreshments. Limited. Friendly ice-cream van (hot drinks available) at Hanover Point.

 Loos. *Shippards Chine:* a small seasonal outpost, recently refurbished (with disabled unit) and bravely maintained in the face of raids by night-revellers who strip the site of anything that might burn on their beastly bonfires.

 Sport. Surfing (for those with boards). Para and hang-gliding on Tapnell Down (tel. 754042).

Walks. Lots in each direction. A classic walk of a couple of miles, to be done any way round, means taking the coastal path from Shippards Chine to Compton Chine and returning along the beach (tide permitting). The clifftop path takes in the few sections of old coastguard road not yet in the sea, including an ageing milestone, and skirts the edges of undercliff carpeted with thrift and patrolled by kestrels. A longer route with exhilarating views, as well as birds and flowers in summer, begins at the car-park beside Afton Down and follows the Freshwater Way up to join the Tennyson Trail eastward over the downs as far as *Five Barrows;* from here, follow the Hamstead Trail down to Brook Bay, where the coastal path leads back to the car-park. You will not be the first to tramp the top section of this route; it was already an ancient ridgeway used by neolithic farmers long before Bronze Age folk came to dig the burial mounds some 3,500 years ago.

Geology. Several gems. The rock formation exposed around Hanover Point continues 5 miles along to Atherfield and reappears at Yaverland; it is the oldest rock visible on the Island and consists mainly of mottled mudstones – brightly coloured marls and clays with bands of sandstone that formed as sediment in a vast shallow lake during the Cretaceous period.

Dinosaurs crossed the mudflats, leaving footprints to sink from sight until revealed by the sea scouring the foreshore west of Hanover Point 120 million years later. Such marks are not easy to spot among the crazy paving of eroded mudstones, but the black remains of wood and vegetation brought down in the floodplain are unmistakeable – as are the logs of the *'Pine Raft'*, visible only at low tide in a hollow 50 yds. short of the sea-mark. Shattered trunks, with growth-rings still discernible, lie turned into stone, the remains of an ancient log-jam dumped in a river delta. Beyond Shippards Chine the rocks change to duller silts and sandstones, marking the approach of a shallow sea; fossil ferns and fishbones are common along the beach, as well as bands of shelly limestone. Towards Compton Chine the cliffs pass through many colours, rivalling Alum Bay, as the succession of Lower Greensand, Gault and Upper Greensand is revealed – deposits formed on the bed of a deepening sub-tropical sea 110 to 95 million years ago. By the end of the bay you have reached the Chalk, accumulated on a sea floor up to 2,000 feet under water. Back at Shippards Chine, the cliff-top is capped with gravel containing bits of twig and hazel. This valley gravel dates back only 7,000 years (Stone Age times), but it marks the course of the Yar – or one of its tributaries – when that river wound through a wide valley and the sea was still a good few miles further south.

Natural History. A prime site. Climb down the path to the west end of Compton beach on a warm June day and you will have no difficulty seeing why this patch of tumbled cliff is special to naturalists. Pink with flowers, the place skips with butterflies – especially the Island's own *Glanville Fritillary*. For reasons not yet understood the I.O.W. is as near as this butterfly ever gets to mainland Britain and the undercliff from Compton and along is its special

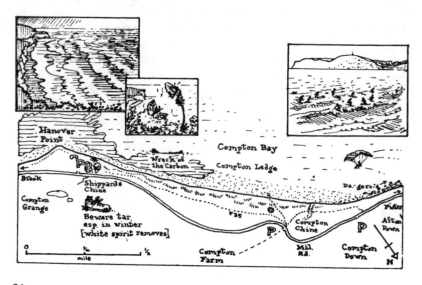

home. The *Glanville Fritillary* (fritillary means 'chequerboard' and Glanville after Lady Eleanor G., 18th century collector extraordinaire) is an attractive insect and photogenic — it stays still on flowers for an obligingly long time. Above Compton the chalk downland is equally good on flora and fauna. Climb up from the car-park by Afton Down and take care where you tread — here grow colonies of orchid (pyramid, common spotted and bee), clustered bellflower, centaury, restharrow and thyme . . . not to mention the occasional lizard.

History. A long past, but little future. 'Comp-ton' is Old English for 'farm in a valley'; that's all the Normans found at Compton when they came by to write up the *Domesday Book* and, 900 years on, that's all there is today. So, too, it should remain, thanks to the good services of the National Trust, who own the area; the Countryside Commission, who have declared it a Heritage Coast, worthy of special protection; and English Nature, who deem the whole coastline down to St Catherine's a Site of Special Scientific Interest. Not that any amount of legislation or good intentions can save Compton from the merciless onslaught of the sea; each year several feet disappear — sometimes yards.

' Dinosaur footprints — '

FRESHWATER BAY

An attractive spot, with something of interest for all ages at any time of year.

P **Access**. Good. Car-parking: SWBC, stone's throw from beach – literally, during winter storms; NT, Afton Down, pleasant 5 min. walk from beach. *Buses*: 1B, 1C, 7 (and it takes 2 hrs from Sandown), 7A, 7C, 17. Level esplanade with ramp and steps on to different ends of beach.

Beach. Mostly pebbles. One sandy corner. Semi-circular bay 300 yards across, cut into chalk cliffs like a bite from a sandwich; south facing, catches plenty of sun – and S.W. breezes – choose your spot to shelter from either. Steep sloping shingle bank round more exposed eastern part of bay; sheltered part round corner from hotel has small sandy patch, held in by anti-tank blocks. Rocky areas at each end of bay. The sea leaves its share of rubbish, which volunteers from the Residents' Association work round the year to shift.

Stag Rock (50 yds out), like others in Europe, was allegedly the last refuge of a stag chased by hounds. Believe that and you'll have no difficulty with the Mermaid Rock, which really did break away only recently – 22 Feb 1969. The famous Arch Rock, for centuries Freshwater's distinctive landmark, collapsed in heavy seas on 25 Oct 1992. At the opposite end of the bay Freshwater Cave (120 ft deep) was a local wonder in the 19th century, but most of it got filled in to strengthen the fort above. The tunnel and steps down were built to give access to the beach by the owners of the ex-fort in 1936.

Bathing. Old guide-books extol the good bathing. However, modern sign warns of 'Steeply Shelving Beach'. Paddlers and small children will prefer the sandy patch. In winter-storms, seas crash over the Albion Hotel.

Safety. Lifebelts at each end of the esplanade and Inshore Rescue Craft (emergency phone alongside) in the middle. Caves at each end of bay can be seen at low spring tides, but don't get cut off trying to reach inaccessible coves beyond. Beware rock dropping from cliffs. The clifftop memorial to E.L.M. (only child, aged 15, lost in 1846) is a sad reminder of the dangers of slithery turf, gusting winds and coastal erosion. The old coastguard road and more recent coastal path have gone into the sea; the new road is due to follow in the next decade.

 Refreshments. Ices at the Mermaid Cafe; drinks and food with a view in the Albion Hotel next door. Good range of food all day at moderate prices at the Tennyson Restaurant. For a cuppa with a view, try the Fort Redoubt Tea-rooms (open when the flag is flying). Queen Victoria had tea here in 1860,

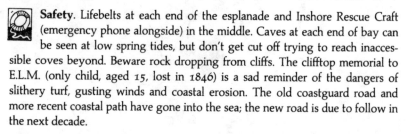

but it was then a fort and the Queen and 4 year old Beatrice were entertained by the colonel's wife.

 Loos. Gate Lane, 100 yds. up from beach. Ancient monument, but reasonably well maintained.

 Sport/Visits. Freshwater Bay Golf Club, superbly positioned, has public Pitch & Putt (752955). West Wight Swimming Pool, Queens Road, Freshwater (752168). Farringford Hotel, open to non-residents for teas, barsnacks and nosing round Tennysonia (752500) Golden Hill Fort, – variable collection of craft-shops etc. Free parking, but watch out for admission charges (753380).

 Walks. *East:* over *Afton Down*, where the sheep still bleat like Bob Dylan – this is the site of the great 1970 I.W. Pop Festival, which few locals will ever forget.

North: variety of circuits round the nature reserve of *Afton Marsh* (muddy at times); then on to the old railway track by the Yar estuary for waders mudflats and the chance of a kingfisher.

West: must be the premier walk on the Island (on a clear day), up to the *Tennyson Monument*, with West Wight spread out beneath you. There's a wide choice of routes, all of them good. The usual way begins in Gate Lane; for a gentler climb take the path up by the thatched church of St. Agnes. The next track along gives a view of the rustic bridge Tennyson put up to avoid admirers on the public footpath below. The shortest route is by the High Down Inn (space for cars in the chalk-pit); the track down from the old Nodes Beacon, on the sheltered side of the down, dances with butterflies in summer sunshine.

 Geology. Stacks. The thickest layer of chalk in Britain is to be found in the Isle of Wight – 1,630 feet of it. But the chalk here is tilted over, like a pack of cards on the slide, as shown by the angled lines of flint that run through the Upper Chalk. The whole formation, built up over more than 25 million years (at less than ¾ inch per thousand years), contains considerable variations within it. This is why the chalk does not erode at an even rate, but makes caves and hollows, leaving arches and pillars, ledges and stacks, each on show in Freshwater. A sill of hard chalk runs across the bay, joining its two ends. When the schooner *Carl* blew ashore in 1916, ending up virtually in the garden of Glenbrook (the crew dropped off the bowsprit on to the lawn), a way back over the ledge had to be blasted with dynamite. Freshwater takes its name from the spring behind the car-park, just 200 yds. from the sea. Within a very short distance the trickle at Afton widens out into the Yar estuary. The sea has broken through to the Yar two or three times this century. In 1916 the flood-waters came near to the ceiling of the level-crossing keeper's cottage by the Causeway.

Natural History. The cliffs around Freshwater are home to birds, notably cormorant and feral dove, but nothing to compare with the past. '... thousands of screaming sea birds darken the chalky sides with dusky plumage.' (1808). Much sport was had by shooting-parties in small boats, who presumably took some care not to hit the locals dangling from ropes to collect eggs and young. Eider down fetched good prices and carcasses baited the crab-pots. However, gentlemen with guns and a taste for guillemot eggs cannot alone be responsible for the depletion of birds here – the decline has continued this century, long after such activities ceased. Puffins, which bred here and could be counted in hundreds around 1900, numbered 30 in 1950 and are now only occasionally sighted, as rare summer visitors. The same goes for Razorbills and Guillemots. But there are still interesting birds in residence along Main Bench – Fulmar, Shag, Great Black-Backed Gull. Nearer to Freshwater, Rock Pipits nest close to the bay, living off flies and sandhoppers that lurk in the seaweed, while Shelduck survey the view from a cliff-top burrow. Here thrive special chalk-loving seaside plants. The things like wild cabbages by the road to Compton are indeed wild cabbage, from which cauliflower and kale are descended. The plant used to be sold in Dover market, but is said to be bitter, unpleasant and in need of much boiling – which could explain school cabbage. Nearby can be found the sweet-scented, pink flowers of the rare Hoary Stock or Gilliflower. Down in the west corner of the bay low tide leaves rocks to scramble over and shallow pools in which to spot small crabs and different forms of anemone.

History. In reality begins with Tennyson. Followed closely by the unstoppable Julia Margaret Cameron. Freshwater attracted most notable visitors – Charles Darwin, Edward Lear, Trollope, Longfellow, Millais, Sullivan, Garibaldi, Lewis Carroll, Prince Albert ... Everybody was somebody in Freshwater Bay, and anybody that wasn't soon became so, thanks to Mrs Cameron's

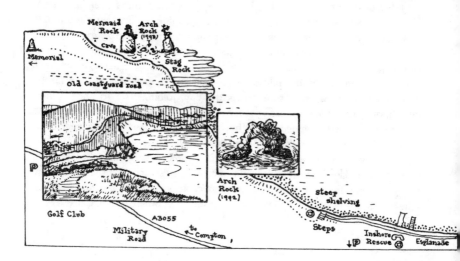

habit of waylaying servants and strangers to pose for her photographs. Kitchen-staff were dressed up as mountain-nymphs. The porter on Yarmouth Pier became King Arthur. A startled Roman Catholic Bishop of Salford just avoided being made the adulterous Sir Lancelot. Only Charles Hay Cameron, Julia's elderly husband, failed to oblige: dressed as Merlin and surrounded by oak-leaves, he found it impossible to stay rigid for the necessary 6 minutes without dissolving into giggles. Between them, the Tennyson and Cameron households set Fresh-water a-buzz with tales of strange goings-on. Farringford is now a hotel, while Dimbola stands awkwardly over the bay, its ivy replaced by seaside paint and walled garden taken over by bungalows.

The cliff-top fort nearby, built in 1855 to keep out the French, was marked on German maps in 1939 as a considerable fortification. However, its only casualties were victims of an artillery accident in 1901, which caused 4 deaths and alleged hauntings to this day. Round the corner is Watcombe Bay, inaccessible from land and scene of a courageous coastguard rescue in 1947. Spare a thought for the 3 men, 1 woman and 2 small girls aboard the *Islay Mist* who made it in a gale up the 350 feet rope cliff-ladder. Not so lucky were the crew of the *War Knight*, which came to rest here in 1918, burnt out after a fearful collision in the Channel. However, the bacon she carried was much appreciated by the locals in time of rationing; other bits of her cargo continued to wash ashore for 50 years.

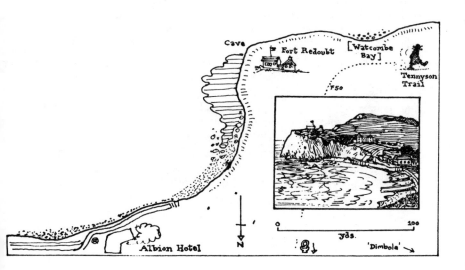

THE NEEDLES HEADLAND

There are no 'beaches' between Freshwater and Alum Bay. Such shoreline as exists at the base of the 400 ft cliffs can be reached only by boat. One corner of the Old Battery gives a tantalising glimpse of Scratchell's Bay with its narrow feint lines of flint in the chalk and Grand Arch, now much eroded. This was the spot chosen by Mr Baldwyn of Lymington for his watery tomb in 1736, having heard his wife swear she would dance on his grave. It was also the scene of a courageous rescue in the January storms of 1890. The *Irex* came to grief on her maiden voyage, carrying 3,500 tons of iron sewage-pipes for Rio de Janeiro. Thirty lives were saved (though one man died soon after), thanks to the rocket-apparatus invented by Mr Dennett of Carisbrooke, the heaving on ropes by men from Golden Hill Fort and the sheer bravery of coastguards and crew who made it up and down the rope in appalling conditions. Last to be saved was the boy Jones, who spent the night alone on board lashed to the mast, too frightened to be coaxed up the cliff.

A large sweep of concrete looks over the scene today, marking the site of Britain's early contributions to the space race. Here in the 1950s, boffins from Saunders-Roe carried out tethered test-firings of the Black Knight rocket, which went on to rise a majestic 300 miles above Woomera, Australia.

Big guns poked out all round the Island's western extremity in the 19th century. When heavy firing was due to take place, a man was sent off on a bicycle to warn the people of Freshwater to keep their windows open – much to the delight of the local burglars. Most of the guns have gone now, but the Battery is still a fine viewpoint for all but claustrophobics – to see The Needles in close-up means walking a 200 ft tunnel bored through the chalk.

The Old Battery was built in 1852, one year before the Tennysons moved into Freshwater. Until overrun with admirers, Farringford was a happy place for Tennyson, inspiring some of his best-loved work – *Maud, Enoch Arden, Idylls of the King*. A towering figure, robust and unkempt, Tennyson knew all the birds and flowers to be found on his vigorous daily tramp over the downs, where 'the sea-wind sang Shrill, chill, with flakes of foam.'

The 482 ft Down is a splendid walk over springy turf, hummocked with remains – neolithic burial-sites and 20th century golf-bunkers, confusingly similar. The poet's memorial, on the site of the Nodes Beacon, is visible in sunshine for miles around. Tennyson Down dominates this part of the Island.

ALUM BAY

The shingle beach is nothing special. Coloured Sands and Needles never disappoint.

Access. Somewhat testing. Two ways down to the beach: walk (234 steps from the Pleasure Park, fewer from the lane at the top) or take the chairlift (80p adult/single). The Needles Pleasure Park advertises itself as free entry, but be prepared for hefty parking-charges in season. Much better, leave the car at Totland or High Down Pit and enjoy the 2 mile walk over Headon Warren or High Down. You won't get better views. *Buses:* 1B, 1C, 17. Or try the 42 from Yarmouth, a vintage open-top bus which corkscrews and wheezes along the clifftop to the Battery.

Beach. Basically upside-down – the soft, loose sand is all in the cliffs, while the beach consists of stone. Tucked in behind the Needles Headland, which gives shelter but also robs it of some winter sun, Alum Bay looks west to Poole Bay and Bournemouth (14 miles off). The view takes in Hengistbury Head and Christchurch, with its tower behind, and, moving right, passes down the Hampshire coast to Barton and Milford. Gone now are the last remains of the old pier (built 1887, partially demolished 1942), on to which visitors thronged off paddle-steamers at the turn of the century. Beyond the new landing-stage the beach consists of 350 yds of coarse, unstable shingle, increasing in gradient towards the corner. Storms sculpt the shingle into mini-bays, with larger stones balanced on loose gravel, down which it is easy to slip into the sea. The slope is gentler in the opposite direction, beyond the steps, where there are sandy patches giving way to a rocky jumble at Hatherwood Point. Tides make little difference here – only 3-4 ft at neaps, which is half the tidal range of the opposite end of the Island. However, low spring tides reveal Five Fingers Rock off Hatherwood and East and West Long rocks in the bay. The beach is one spot from which the Pleasure Park is not visible.

Bathing. The water-quality should be good here, being well away from any outfall. Care should be taken, as strong tidal currents swirl into the bay, making bathing hazardous.

Safety. The main danger is posed by the loose sand in the cliffs. Do not on any account be tempted into scrambling up or dig into these – the many warning-signs date back to a particularly poignant tragedy.

Refreshments/Loos. Kiosks, cafes, restaurant, bar at the Pleasure Park, which caters for half a million mouths a year. Alternatively there is Alum Bay Tearooms, which lays claim to The Best View on the Island. Loos can be found in the Pleasure Park complex – clean and good, with hot water.

Entertainment/Sport. Carousel, rides and amusements at the Pleasure Park. Gentler souls will prefer the fill-your-own sand-shape shop. Pitch and Putt at the Tearooms. Crazy Golf round the Pleasure Park. Anglers on boats out of Yarmouth do a good line in cod (34lbs) off the Needles. Boat trips round the bay in summer – interesting to discover tunnels and trapdoors in the chalk cliff.

Visits. Alum Bay Glass (753473, open all year) – fascinating to watch items take shape. An appropriate spot to make glass, as large amounts of Alum Bay sand in the last century (22,000 tons between 1850-5) were shipped out through Yarmouth to Bristol and London to be turned into goblets and greenhouses. The particular sand – fine, white and soft as flour – can still be seen in patches along the top of the beach to the right of the steps. The Needles Pleasure Park (752401, open Easter – Oct) is the Island's answer to Land's End.

Walks. "Of all 'beauty-spots' I have seen," wrote John Betjeman, "Alum Bay is the most certainly entitled to be called beautiful." That was before the chairlift. Best seen from a boat and in afternoon sun after rain, the sands still look good from the road which leads to the Old Battery. It's a brisk and bracing 20 mins. to the Battery, but allow time for detours on the way. Headon Warren (T17) has views just as good; the Bronze Age burial-mound at the top, is a vantage-point for distant Dorset and a full sweep down the Solent. Stick to the paths; thick undergrowth and the rough terrain deter all progress off the beaten track.

Geology. Stunning in all directions. First the Needles, which are the hard stumps of chalk ridge extending to Dorset, with its own fine Old Harry Rocks. The sea broke through perhaps 10,000 years ago, leaving buoys and a sinister line of rough water to mark the run of underwater pinnacles that has claimed many wrecks. There were once more Needles – and needle-like rocks – than now. The last main one to go was Lot's Wife, or Cleopatra's Needle, a 120 ft pillar which crashed down in 1764.

The Coloured Sands: hard to believe sometimes that the neat boxes of pastel-hued sand in the shop have all come straight from the cliff below . . . but Nature really has flung the paint-pot at this motley patch. Mineral impurities turn the colourless quartz into sand of 21 shades in five main colours – red, white, yellow, green and black. The individual layers of sand were formed under shallow seas some 50 million years ago and then pushed upright by the great geological shudder that formed the Alps. To either side of the sands are beds of clay so rich in perfect fossils that it is easy to understand the errors of 18th century writers, who believed these were recent shells thrown up by stormy seas, embedded in the cliff and petrified by salt.

Natural History. Wildlife tends to lurk round the blind side of the Needles. However, a visit to the Old Battery might bring you nose to beak with a Greater Black-backed Gull (2ft 6ins from tip to tail).

 History. Alum Bay takes its name from the powdery yellow efflorescence that still appears on the cliffs. Alum, used as a fixative in dyeing, was extracted in the 16th century, until coal-shales were found to be a cheaper source. Of the many wrecks that foundered on the Needles two stand out: HMS *Assurance* (1753), which hit Goose rock just NW of the lighthouse, and SS *Varvassi*, whose cargo of oranges and wine brightened the austere days of January 1947. The present lighthouse dates from 1859. It has cellars deep in the rock and an unevenly stepped base, optimistically designed to prevent waves sweeping up and over, some 110 feet. Uglified by the recent addition of a helipad, the lighthouse is being prepared for automation, perhaps in 1994. The date has been put back a good many times: since 1987 Yarmouth lifeboat on its Christmas run to the lighthouse has carried a 'last trip' memorial plaque. The previous lighthouse, high on the down, was invariably hidden in sea mist at the times it was most needed. Fitting, though, that Marconi should have chosen Alum Bay for some of his earliest experiments with radio communication (1897-1900) as commemorated by the memorial in the car-park.

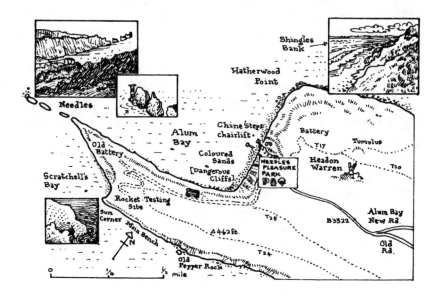

TOTLAND BAY

Pleasant, family beach with quiet, old-fashioned air; emptier than Colwell, but enjoyed by locals.

Access. Immediate. Step down off the esplanade, which has just one or two spaces for parking. Much safer, especially in summer, to leave the car at the top and walk the couple of minutes down by the road or steps from the Turf Walk. *Buses*: 1B, 1C, 7, 7A, 42 – get out by the War Memorial.

Beach. Firm sand below and beyond the rim of shingle. West facing, Totland gives views of the Dorset and Hampshire coastline. High tide laps close to the sea-wall, leaving a steepish bank of stones, which is somewhat misleading. Below and to the west is clean sand at a shallow gradient. 1993 sees major coastal defence works taking place at Totland, either side of the pier, with 'beach-nourishment' promised.

Bathing. Good. Safe, calm water in a sheltered bay. Some problems recently, especially at weekends, with motor-boats and water-skiers speeding in the bay, in contravention of the 200m limit set down in local bye-laws. Water-quality good: EC tests passed with flying colours over the last five years.

Safety. Reasonable – take care by the groynes. More of a hazard, perhaps, is traffic along the sea-wall/esplanade, which appears from nowhere and spatters pebbles on to sunbathers below.

Refreshments. The Waterfront Licensed Restaurant & Cafe (754130) is open all year, providing hot and cold food from eleven in the morning to ten at night.

Loos. Totland's Eurobogs, close to the pier, welcome visitors in three languages during the season. Those at the Recreation Ground stay open all year.

Entertainment. In new hands and undergoing restoration, the pier at present has a small amusement area. It was originally built as a landing-stage and promenade for the prosperous and genteel classes coming from the mainland. Early August is the time for Freshwater and Totland carnival.

Sport. Bowls at The Broadway (754314); swimming at West Wight Pool, Queens Road, Freshwater (752168). Totland Bay with its mixture of sand and rocks (Tinker Shoal off the pier and Penner Rocks towards Hatherwood) makes for good fishing – bass, conger, sole . . .

Walks. 'Totland' means look-out point and 'Warden', along the sea-wall to Colwell, means watch-hill. Ships heading south down the Solent from Southampton save 10 miles by going this way round the Island, but they need to be vessels drawing less than 9.5m. Headon Warren, 397 ft up, gives a commanding view of the route and is a nice point from which to see the early stages of the Round the Island race in June or the Cowes-Torquay powerboats in August. To get there from the beach, follow the old smugglers' path (T33) up Widdick Chine, by the former lifeboat-house; from the top it's just half a mile along the road and well-marked paths on to the Warren.

Geology. Good fossils in the rocks beyond the old lifeboat-station. The Headon Beds are relatively recent in geological terms (37 million years or so), but none the less interesting for that. Blocks of sandy brown limestone along the beach contain nice examples of freshwater snails, like Galba and the neatly spiralled Planorbina, shaped like a Catherine-wheel.

Natural History. With its acid gravel cap and sandy scrub land, Headon (the name means heather-hill) stands in marked contrast to the neighbouring ridge of chalk downland over which Tennyson strode. Good for rabbits and birds – warblers, redstarts, goldcrests, if you're lucky. Paths twist over Headon, ending as ever in the remains of a Victorian battery

History. Likened, perhaps unfairly, by Betjeman to 'Bromley by the sea', Totland has a distinctly Home Counties feel, with its Scots pines and tiled turrets, all the work of one architect. Gone is the grand hotel boasting 'seawater baths', but the village still has many small pockets of interest. The church gate fought at Trafalgar, only in those days it was part of the timber that

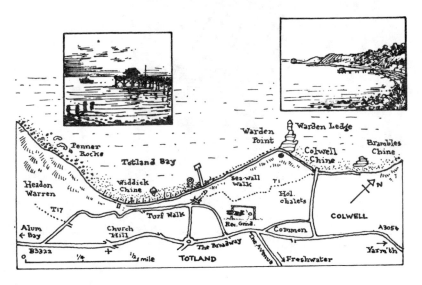

formed HMS *Thunderer*. Aman Court commemorates the local man behind one of many Solent Tunnel Schemes that failed to get under the ground. At beach level, Totland Bay was landing-point and mason's yard for the stone that made the Needles lighthouse. The brick building at the west end of the beach is the old lifeboat station. On the far side of it is fixed a rather dated and weatherworn board explaining Totland Tides in splendid doggerel:

When full or new
You see the Moon,
The tide's far out
In the afternoon.

But when the Moon's
At either quarter,
At tea the beach
Is under water . . .

COLWELL

Cheap 'n cheerful, W. Wight's answer to Sandown.

 Access. Good, down Colwell Chine Rd, with all amenities within a few yards of beach. *Car-parking:* SWBC long-stay at end of Chine Rd, with some free spaces for overflow along Colwell Common Rd. *Buses:* 7, 7A, 17, 42 from Yarmouth stop along Common.

 Beach. Can fill up especially at HT when the beach all but disappears. Colwell's Long Beach offers a good strip of firm sand at low water in a relatively sheltered bay facing NW. The view to Hampshire takes in Hurst Castle (1¼ miles òff) with its lighthouse and yachting hazard, The Trap, and runs west along Hurst Point to Milford (3½m) and Barton (6m). Midway, the Shingles Bank can sometimes be seen raising its head from the bed of the Solent. Colwell Bay sweeps round ¾ mile from Warden Point to Fort Albert, with a third rocky ledge (How Bank) running out from the middle. The beach has a gentle slope of clean sand beneath a rim of gravel, which beyond Brambles Chine turns into more steeply shelving shingle, with blocks of concrete and rusted iron. The beach ends with rocks by Linstone Chine and private land beyond. The coastal battery at Fort Warden is no longer a holiday-camp; but from here to the chalets falling over the cliff at Brambles (15 years ago there was a field in between), there is self-catering accommodation of every kind – serving the traditional, low-budget family holiday. All this can make for a crowded beach, especially when the tide is up and lapping at the esplanade, where it stays for 2 hrs. (except at neaps) in this part of the Island. *Dogs* – prohibited (May-Sept) from Colwell Chine to Warden Point. Along the sea-wall leads are compulsory and mess must be removed.

 Bathing. Good swimming and (except at HW) good paddling for small children. Best in centre between the beacons (avoiding area round slipway, concrete footings etc.). Beyond the sea-wall towards Ft Albert two sections of beach between groynes enclose the weed-covered rocky platform of How Ledge, which runs out to sea, along with several storm drains. Colwell has passed minimum EC bathing-water tests over the last five years.

 Safety. Good. Activities in the water under the eye of local longshoreman and assistants, with fast boat on hand, should the need arise. Keep a safe distance from the unstable low cliffs towards Brambles Chine and beyond.

 Refreshments/Loos. Plenty, within yards of beach, including the new Beachside Cafe. The Captain's Cabin is open all hours, wafting odours of breakfast and chips. The general stores/off-licence nearby provides an alternative supply of nibbles and ices. (Together they stock a pretty unbeatable range of cheap 'beach-goods'.) The loos are conveniently placed, if somewhat cheerless. Open all year, with disabled unit. (Loos also along cliff path at Recreation Ground, Totland.)

 Entertainment. Amusements, pool etc. at Reception block to Sunset Complex (by car-park). Not far along the cliff-path west (TI) is Totland Recreation Ground, with swings and space for children.

 Sport/Hire. Wide range of equipment available for water-sports at own risk, e.g. canoes, pedaloes, motorboats and windsurfing with or without tuition and wetsuit. Deckchairs, sunloungers, windbreaks at reasonable prices. Limited no. of beach-huts.

Walks. Short and sweet. The sea-wall west round Warden Pt (with a nice view of the Needles) makes an easy, level walk to Totland (½m), suitable for wheeling, except when winter seas crash over. The cliff-path back zig-zags along ways much visited by dogs banned from the beach. In the other direction severe erosion at Brambles Chine and private ownership around Ft Albert oblige the coastal path to take twists and turns inland before the way down to Ft Victoria can be reached – but it's worth at least rounding the bay to Brambles for the fine view west.

Geology. Around 35 million years ago this area consisted of tropical swamps and lagoons, which have been likened to the Florida Everglades. Deceased shellfish kept rather well in the mud and Victorian collectors flocked here to marvel at the preservation of the shells in Colwell's Venus and Oyster Beds. These are still to be seen in certain patches of exposed cliff towards and around Brambles Chine.

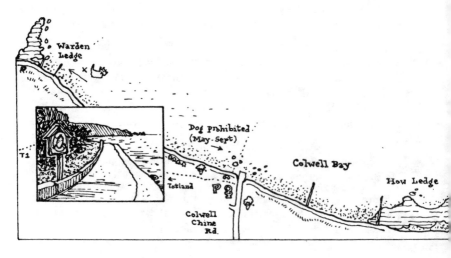

Natural History. Watch out for the sign of sand-masons along the water's edge at low tide — a forest of little chimneys made from sand and shell, each the work of a DIY-mad worm lurking up to 1ft. down in the sand. When the tide comes in, it puts out feelers to net in what goodies may come its way.

History. Apart from tales of the smuggling Conway brothers, most of Colwell's history relates to its role as a military encampment. In Napoleonic times 150 men were camped on the Common, with Rockstone Cottage in use as officers' mess. French scares continued through the century and Colwell's slipway was built to unload the heavy cannon brought in to fortify the Freshwater peninsula. Funny to think therefore that Fort Albert was built at a time (1854-6) when Britain and France were actually together on the same side in the Crimean War. (Fort Warden followed, by way of extra precaution, in 1862.) As elsewhere, Fort Albert was already obsolete within a few years of its completion, such was the rapid development of naval firepower in the 19th century. However, it took on a new role in 1885 as testing-station for the Navy's hush-hush new weapon, the Brennan torpedo. Finally abandoned in 1956, Fort Albert has been converted into luxury flats, suitable for those keen on taking up musical instruments: the outer walls are 11ft thick at the base.

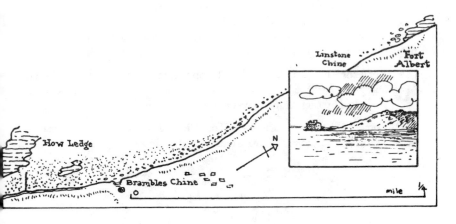

FORT VICTORIA
TO YARMOUTH

Plenty of interest in and around Yarmouth, but bathing only at Norton.

Access. Level walk from all directions. No parking in the immediate vicinity of Norton; ½ mile back over the river is the main car-park in Yarmouth. Better, drive on to Fort Victoria with free parking and enjoy the ¼ mile walk back along the sea-wall. *Buses: 7, 7A, 17, 42 to Yarmouth.*

Beach. Sandhard Beach at Norton is a small strip of sloping shingle with a scattering of sand, buoyed off to keep out the many small craft around. Dog ban under review. Rocks and weed prevail along the sea-wall to Fort Victoria, beyond which the shoreline opens out into beach again – shallow shelving with patches of sand, much strewn with weed.

Bathing. Not an EC designated beach, Norton has nevertheless been monitored and passed for the last five years. The long rope keeps out water-skiers, but not all sewage: Yarmouth sewage is a long-running issue. Absolutely no bathing at Fort Victoria, for reasons given below under 'Safety'.

Safety. Sandhard Beach is safe enough, unlike the waters just off it, with the strong ebb-tide out of the harbour, Black Rock (mostly hidden) and Fiddlers Race just beyond. The lifeboat nearby, with its distinguished record of gallantry and rescue, makes a reassuring presence in the harbour.
Fort Victoria: to get through Hurst Narrows the otherwise shallow Solent has gouged a channel 31 fathoms (186 ft) deep. The current here runs at 4-5 knots. It's a good spot for landlubbers in garden-chairs to watch small boats battle against what the poet Drayton in 1622 described as -
  Those rough ireful tides as in her straights they meet
  With boisterous shocks and roars each other rudely greet.
The coastguard puts it no less colourfully, warning that anyone foolish enough to enter these waters would soon be in France with no passport.

Refreshment. Fort Victoria has the Spinnaker Cafe, as well as barbecue and picnic facilities. Along the sea-wall by Yarmouth a tempting barbecue is worked by chefs at the Wayfarer Cafe (in season).

Loos. Well fortified facilities at Fort Victoria in former gun casemates. Bridge Rd, Yarmouth (all year), Norton Spit in season.

Entertainment. Yarmouth is a small town with a community-minded populace, strong on traditional pancake races, sports on the green and bonfire nights, all for good causes. The Carnival in mid-August packs in activities from Punch & Judy to crabbing competitions on the harbour-wall.

Sport. The Savoy Leisure Centre (760355, weekly membership available to non-residents) has sporting facilities second to none and a fine record in providing opportunities for people of all ages and abilities. Water-Sports: along the sea-wall by Norton, with equipment on hire for windsurfing, canoeing, water-skiing etc.

Visits. Yarmouth Castle was built around 1549, just after the French had burnt the town for the second time, and is open from Easter to October (760678). Fort Victoria (760283) is a place surprisingly little used by locals. At first glance somewhat dilapidated (it is, after all, a ruin), the site has a good deal to offer, including Sea Life Aquarium and exhibitions of marine archaeology – both seasonal and both you pay for, but the park with its walks and views is freely open all year. Planetarium now open.

Walks. At Fort Victoria the country park trail follows the old Military Road up through the woods to Cliff End Fort and views of the Needles. (For a closer look, watch out for 1½ hour boat-trips in the summer from Yarmouth Pier). Between Forts Albert and Victoria the path opens out to give views of Hurst, barely one mile off, where Charles 1st spent a dismal last Christmas in 1648.

Natural History. Norton Spit has sea-lavender on the mud-flats and attractive flowers of striped sea-bindweed and sea-holly in the dunes. Prickly, but not a holly, this plant is a member of the parsley family, whose roots were candied and eaten as sweets in Tudor times. The Oglanders of Nunwell recommended it as a cure for consumption, chopped up with 30 snails and 30 earthworms, all washed down with a quart of milk – from a red cow.

History. The headland has always had some kind of fortification. Fort Victoria, built 1852-3, was a Palmerstonian folly, outdated even before its completion. Used as a searchlight base (and military training depot up to 1962), Fort Victoria proved of greatest use in 1908, when its personnel assisted in the rescue of men off *HMS Gladiator*, rammed by a liner in a snowstorm off Yarmouth. Twenty-seven drowned.

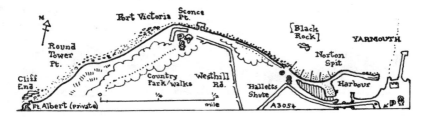

YARMOUTH
BOULDNOR

Stretch of coastline with nothing for beachgoers,
lots for the naturalist.

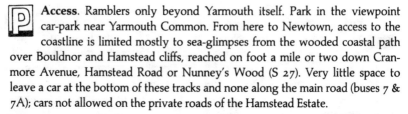

 Access. Ramblers only beyond Yarmouth itself. Park in the viewpoint car-park near Yarmouth Common. From here to Newtown, access to the coastline is limited mostly to sea-glimpses from the wooded coastal path over Bouldnor and Hamstead cliffs, reached on foot a mile or two down Cranmore Avenue, Hamstead Road or Nunney's Wood (S 27). Very little space to leave a car at the bottom of these tracks and none along the main road (buses 7 & 7A); cars not allowed on the private roads of the Hamstead Estate.

 Safety. Landslips and mudflows. Very soft ground around the slumping cliffs and blue-slipper clay by the Ledges have trapped the occasional holidaymaker. The memorial at Hamstead to three young men lost at sea here in the 1930s is a sad reminder of the strength of the ebb-tides that rip out of Newtown and Yarmouth Harbours.

 Refreshments/Loos. Busy all summer, with more than 4,500 boats visiting the harbour till full each August, Yarmouth has enough cafes and hostelries to make pub-crawling literally possible. Eastwards, nothing till Shalfleet. Loos at the Common at Yarmouth (all year, with disabled unit).

 Entertainments. Watch out in mid-August for the Newtown Randy, a one-day festival of fund-raising and rural pursuits more innocent, perhaps, than the name might suggest.

Visits. At Newtown the lopsided Old Town Hall with its local interest display is opened on certain days by the National Trust. Further along, Clamerkin Farm Park (78396) has animals and things to appeal to all ages.

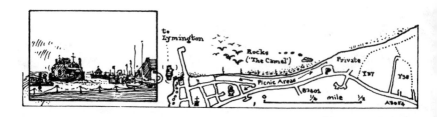

Walks. Allow plenty of time for the five-mile Hamstead loop, best done in good summer weather. Follow the Hamstead Estate Road (S 27) over the tail-end of Ningwood Lake, past Hamstead Grange. Beyond Hamstead Farm the path drops down to the shore. Turning homeward, the path skirts marshland and mudflat in a series of mini-causeways and bridges, before striking dry land again at Lower Hamstead with its jetty.

Geology. Bouldnor and Hamstead are rich in fossil fauna and the only place in the world where oligocene formations of a certain age are obligingly exposed by the sea.

Natural History. Good in summer, when footpaths through the Hamstead meadows are alive with small butterflies, and the shingle bank of Hamstead Spit has yellow horned poppy and white splashes of sea-kale in flower against the background carpet of rich pink thrift. Back over Bouldnor, the clay soils play unexpected host to chalk-loving plants, duped by the rich layers of ancient shells deposited in the cliff.

History. Bouldnor clays gave rise to quite an industry in local brickmaking. Visible from the coastal path (S 1) are the remains of the stone pier where bricks were loaded in the 19th century. Nearby on the Hamstead estate, Regency architect John Nash devised local employment schemes which included brickworks and horse-drawn railway. No less colourful a character was Sir Robert Holmes of Yarmouth (his cheekily botched memorial is in the church). Soldier of fortune, slave-trader and downright pirate, Holmes was responsible for naming New York and adding guineas to the coinage. The sea bed off Yarmouth has yielded many interesting finds: Tudor wrecks, Roman pottery, and even flint axes and vegetation in the peat which pre-dates the flooding of the Solent and severance of the Island (complete by 6,000 BC.)

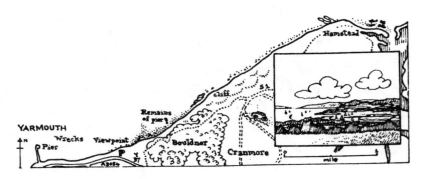

NEWTOWN

Not new, not a town and certainly no beach, Newtown is nonetheless a place of enormous fascination to all who enjoy history and nature. Once a busy port capable of sheltering fifty ships of 500 tons, Newtown was sacked by the French in 1377 and, happily, never recovered. Grass grew over the remains of shops and streets, still visible today, but as a Rotten Borough Newtown went on sending two members to Parliament till 1832. The Duke of Marlborough was one of them.

The harbour has silted up, the pastures flooded and salterns abandoned, leaving a carpet of mud picked over by birds of every description. The mudflats are packed with shellfish and small creatures, yielding as much as a ton of food per acre. Don boots and follow the footpath (CB 9) from Gold Street over a field and causeway to the windswept quay and marshland left bare by the tide. Don't count on seeing the osprey or the white stork recently spotted, but set your sights instead on the black-tailed godwit, the ringed and golden plover and the winter flocks of Brent Geese beating past.

Alternatively park beyond the New Inn at Shalfleet and walk the ¾ mile track (CB 12) to another quay in the estuary, crowded in winter with lapwing and curlew, wigeon and teal.

A million people live within a mile of the Solent and its waters are busy with traffic. But the Solent estuaries provide a habitat of international importance. Each winter 150,000 wildfowl and waders fly in to stick their beaks in this mud. A quarter of the world's Dark-Bellied Brent Geese overwinter in these estuaries, which are home to various threatened species. Among them, the rare but delightfully named Insensible Shrimp, which lurks in Newtown lagoons.

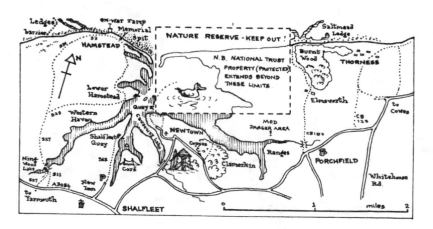

BURNT WOOD

There's just one way down to the shore between Newtown and Thorness, a 1¼ mile walk from Porchfield, which brings you down to a patch of mud and stones by Saltmead Ledge. For the discreet naturalist it's a pleasant ramble through quiet countryside, but forget it if you're a dedicated beachgoer, setting forth with deckchair, windbreak, cool-box and barbecue. This is not a beach.

Take the lane north from the war-memorial at Porchfield, which soon crosses Rodge Brook, a muddy stream still tidal at this point – hence the large shore crab often to be seen lurking beneath the bridge. Past the kennels, the footpath (CB 1) continues through Elmsworth Farm and along two sides of Burnt Wood, to finish up at the water's edge in a tangle of seaweed, shells and boating litter. Catch it in the right light, with the Solent an irridescent green beneath lowering skies and with the lap and swish of the tide broken only by the plaintive piping of oyster-catchers, and you appreciate the importance of keeping this stretch of coastline unspoilt and unvisited. This is National Trust property, kept strictly for the birds. From the shore there is only one direction to go and that is back the way you came.

Winter waders . . .

THORNESS

Quiet shoreline, best appreciated by summer sail-boarders and winter waders.

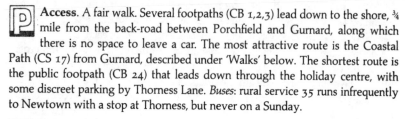

Access. A fair walk. Several footpaths (CB 1,2,3) lead down to the shore, ¾ mile from the back-road between Porchfield and Gurnard, along which there is no space to leave a car. The most attractive route is the Coastal Path (CS 17) from Gurnard, described under 'Walks' below. The shortest route is the public footpath (CB 24) that leads down through the holiday centre, with some discreet parking by Thorness Lane. *Buses*: rural service 35 runs infrequently to Newtown with a stop at Thorness, but never on a Sunday.

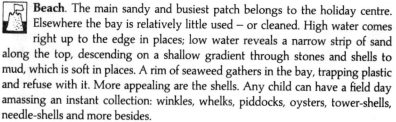

Beach. The main sandy and busiest patch belongs to the holiday centre. Elsewhere the bay is relatively little used – or cleaned. High water comes right up to the edge in places; low water reveals a narrow strip of sand along the top, descending on a shallow gradient through stones and shells to mud, which is soft in places. A rim of seaweed gathers in the bay, trapping plastic and refuse with it. More appealing are the shells. Any child can have a field day amassing an instant collection: winkles, whelks, piddocks, oysters, tower-shells, needle-shells and more besides.

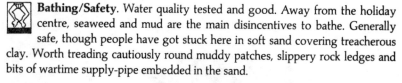

Bathing/Safety. Water quality tested and good. Away from the holiday centre, seaweed and mud are the main disincentives to bathe. Generally safe, though people have got stuck here in soft sand covering treacherous clay. Worth treading cautiously round muddy patches, slippery rock ledges and bits of wartime supply-pipe embedded in the sand.

Refreshments/Loos. No public facilities of any kind in the immediate surroundings – everything belongs to the Holiday Park. No loos.

Sport. Plenty of choice for riding in the area, with stables at Thorness Bay (521357), Porchfield (Romany, 525467) and Comforts Farm, Northwood (293888).

Visits. Calbourne Mill (Calb. 227) combines a fine old mill with a splendid assortment of bygones and 'gosh-I-remember-thoses'. If heading down Forest Road out of Newport, children will appreciate a stop-off at the Donkey Sanctuary (821593), where admission is free every afternoon and donations gratefully received.

Walks. The Coastal Trail (CS 17) to Thorness is a 1¾ mile cliff-top stroll, good on butterflies and orchids in summer, blackberries in autumn and mud in winter. The path gives grand views down the Solent to one side (from the far side of Southampton Water, 7 miles off, down 9 miles of water to Hurst) and curious glimpses of home-made chalets and converted railway-carriages to the other. Don't try rounding this coastline at shore-level — rough boulders, impenetrable scrub and private property rule this out.

Geology. Here, as elsewhere along the Hamstead coast, may be found along the shore rich clusters of beautifully formed fossil shells. In the low bank along the Gurnard end of Thorness Bay can be seen the tightly packed, fine-grained, creamy stone, which is the source of the delicate insect impressions admired by visitors to the Geology Museum at Sandown.

Natural History. Botanists will enjoy the variety of flowers with shingle plants in the bay (sea aster, sea rocket, sea purslane, seablite, sea spur-rey), and marsh flowers in the former salterns behind. Birds are plentiful. Plovers, dunlin, oyster-catchers and turnstones pick over the receding tide, while wigeon and mallard stay out to sea. At the water's edge it is not unusual here to find large numbers of jellyfish washed up.

History. 210 years ago from this spot you might have looked out 3 miles to the opposite shore and seen Nelson's *Agamemnon* sail out of the Beaulieu River on her maiden voyage. In more recent memory Thorness itself played a critical part in a still greater naval-military enterprise, as training-ground for the Normandy landings. Still visible at low tide are the remains of pipes which brought oil ashore here, to be pumped across the Island and thence by pipeline under the ocean (PLUTO) to power the D-Day invasion. The large red-chequered board in Thorness Bay is a measured-distance post for ships leaving port to calibrate their equipment by; its other half is one nautical mile down the coast by Clamerkin. Yellow boards from Thorness to Cowes warn shipping of gas-mains, telephone and electricity cables across to the mainland. There are even two large pipes on the sea-bed carrying water from the River Test.

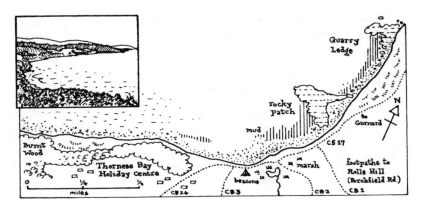

GURNARD

A pleasant spot to sit and watch the world sail by.

Access. Immediate access off the Esplanade at Woodvale, reached either from Cowes or via Gurnard Heights. Alternatively, join the shore at Marsh Road, or pick your way down the low bank into Cook's Bay from the beginning of the Coastal Path (CS 16) just above. Free parking at Woodvale, but little room for cars by Marsh Road. *Buses*: Service 4.

Beach. Has seen better days.

Woodvale: once a prime spot with its Edwardian regattas and changing tents and still popular in 1974 'owing to its bracing climate and good bathing'. The pontoons have now gone and so has much of the sand — despite the construction of groynes of loose rock to coax it back. The present beach, which has little to show at high water, consists of a narrow strip of shelly sand, sloping gently down through stones, with patches of clay exposed, to the lower levels of silty sand with a scattering of rocks. Woodvale looks west to Hengistbury Head (18m) and across two miles of water to Lepe.

Marsh Road: the foreshore here is little more than mud and stones, mixed in with rubble. Rightly or not, Solent dredging has been blamed for the loss of beach. Little hint now of former glories, such as the Roman Villa, the busy quay or the spot where Charles II, Prince Rupert and the Duke of York came ashore in 1671.

Cook's Bay: small stony bay, strewn with debris, boulders, litter and wrack.

Dogs: the local council is at present seeking Home Office approval for a May-Sept. ban on dogs from the main sections of beach at Woodvale and Gurnard Marsh.

Bathing. Water-quality a problem here with recent tests failed, despite new treatment works and improvement scheme.

Safety. Keep clear of the rough groynes and scattered concrete blocks. Otherwise safe, though complaints have been voiced over sailboarders and small craft ignoring regulations and people bathing.

Refreshments. Water's Edge (292043) family restaurant offers coffee, snacks and evening meals in season. The views over the Solent are shared by the Woodvale Inn, just above.

Loos. New block (with disabled unit) where the beach-huts meet Shore Road: clean, well-serviced and open all year — hot water even in January.

Sport. The public slipway at Gurnard attracts a fair number of sailboarders, small yachts and, some would say, late-night noise.

 Hire. Visitors are welcome to the putting-green, when in operation (equipment from Hut 7). Most of the huts are leased out by the council, but one is available to let on a daily or weekly basis.

 Walks. A level, if bracing, ¾ mile along Princes Esplanade to Cowes. Built by unemployed workers, the esplanade was opened by the Prince of Wales, later Duke of Windsor, in 1926. Fifty yards out at Egypt Point is entombed a German bomber brought down in World War II.

 Natural History. The overgrown coastal strip from Gurnard to Cowes is still home to foxes and much other wild-life.

 History. Gurnard's heyday was earlier in the century, when it prospered as a bathing-spot for the populations of Newport and Cowes. Now somewhat poor relations, Gurnard's residents feel understandably aggrieved at the rundown state of local amenities, in contrast with the showpiece of Ryde. Gurnard may have lost its sand, but its assets still are magnificent sunsets and public-spirited local benefactors.

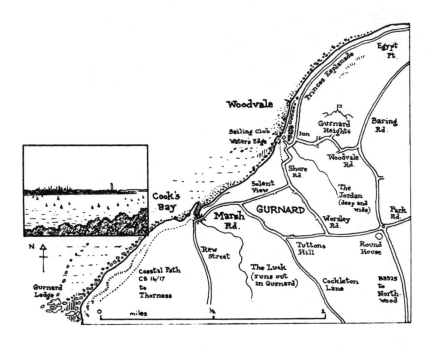

WEST COWES

Poor beach, splendid viewpoint – plenty to amuse the idle spectator.

P **Access**. Immediate access from the esplanade, which runs all the way to Gurnard. Only the first half-mile, below Princes Green, could ever be deemed beach, but the remaining mile is road with free parking, well filled on the occasions when Fastnet racers, Tall Ships, power-boats and Round-the-World yachtsmen sweep by. *Buses*: 1A, 2, 3, 4 to Cowes Bus Station.

Beach. Bank of rather sharp stones (with weed and litter) sloping down to rocks. Large vessels swinging round the deep-water channel into Southampton Water add interest to the view (pay telescope) of worried yachtsmen being swept backwards by the tide, unable to make it round the corner into Cowes. Passing ships also cause unexpected large waves. Dog restrictions currently being drafted.

Bathing. Once a prime spot, with diving-rafts and swimming-sports, but now not a beach to recommend for bathing. Tourist- and water-board bosses swam here, the local MP drank the water and all three lived to tell the tale, but EC tests have been badly failed in Cowes for the last 5 years. Southern Water is spending £13 million on a massive scheme replacing 15-odd river and seafront outfalls with one long pipe and treatment works at Old Castle Point. Strong tidal streams close inshore.

Safety. Currents, liner-wash and sewage apart, the beach is not especially unsafe – unlike the harbour, where local children place themselves in serious danger by defying the signs and diving in. Cowes Harbour has more than 10,000 ferry movements a year. For those who do get into difficulties, Cowes Rescue operate an inshore service from E. Cowes (covering Gurnard to Fishbourne). The volunteers (reached by 999 calls) provide 24 hour cover throughout the year and a watch is kept at weekends.

Loos. The Parade and Northwood Park; Mornington Green and The Cut (behind the Parade bandstand) both include disabled unit.

Entertainment. For eight days a year, Cowes is Cowes, with all that that entails – sailing, drinks and loud voices from upstairs windows. Cowes Week (timed to follow the Goodwood Races) proceeds in early August, with carnival, bands and a host of like attractions in its wake. It always ends with a bang, courtesy of the Council-funded Grand Fireworks Display on Friday night.

Sport. Golf at the club (292303); putting, bowls and croquet in Northwood Park (293974); but it is of course sailing that brings people to Cowes. Beginners can learn at places like the UK Sailing Centre (294941). More than 800 boats compete in the 25 races a day of Cowes Week, but racing extends from May to Sept. with a continuous fixture-list of regattas and championships among the 69 affiliated clubs of the Solent Cruising and Racing Association. The climax is reached every other year (odd years) with the Admiral's Cup Series, culminating in the departure of the Fastnet Race. June, meanwhile, sees more than 1,500 boats set off Round the Island, the fastest trimarans getting back in under four hours.

Visits. Cowes Library & Maritime Museum (Beckford Road) gives free admission to a small display of local interest, centred on Uffa Fox, creator of historic craft, from the airborne lifeboat to that in which John Ridgeway rowed the Atlantic. Fox's most endearing memorial is the event which takes place in mid-Solent each September, when the Brambles Bank is briefly exposed by equinoctial tides to allow a cricket match to take place between two local yacht clubs. Ducks are not unknown.

Walks. The Parade is *the* place to saunter. Most people pause beneath the balcony of the Royal Yacht Squadron, to eavesdrop on what may well be the most exclusive club in the world. Don't linger too long if racing is in progress: more than 1,200 ear-splitting rounds are let off in Cowes Week by the miniature cannon arrayed by the starting-line. The 22 cannon came from a model man o'war built for William IV's children to use on Virginia Water. Cruises in season (around the harbour, Spitbank, Portsmouth etc.) from the Parade by Solent & Wight Line (64602).

History. Cowes Front is rich in memories of its former glories – from Rosetta Cottage, where Jennie Jerome fell for Randolph Churchill, to the drinking-fountain given by George Stephenson, nephew of the 'Rocket' builder. Plaques on the bandstand commemorate such events as the sailing of the *Dove* and the *Ark* to America in 1633 and the 1942 air-raid, when the Polish destroyer *Blyskawica* fought all night to save the town. But it is in the boatyards of Cowes that most history has been made – lifeboats and destroyers, submarines and paddle-steamers, speedboats and biplanes, flying-boats and hovercraft.

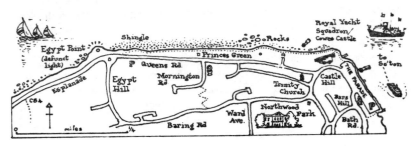

LAWS AND CODES

Far from being areas of no man's land where anything goes, beaches are protected by a battery of legislation guarding rights of ownership and controlling the activities of all who venture on the sands. Every inch of beach and everything found upon it belongs ultimately to someone.

'Can I Take It Home?' The answer is probably 'No'. Things washed up are subject to complex laws of salvage and wreck. No matter how they got into the sea, items of value that come ashore should be reported to the local Receiver of Wreck (HM Customs, Cowes, 293132). Needless to say, he will not be too pleased to be informed of every piece of driftwood that arrives on the beach.

Similar discretion is called for when it comes to material forming a beach. It is an offence to take pebbles, shells, sand, rocks or seaweed from any beach, 'public' or not. This all belongs to the owner of that part of the beach. Her Majesty will no doubt be kind enough to look the other way in the case of a pocketful of pebbles or child's collection of shells, but anyone carting off rocks, sand or gravel in any quantity will end up in deep water.

Fossils are legally the property of whoever has the mineral rights to where they are found – usually the landowner. Those taken from above the High Water Mark without the owner's express permission leave the collector open to charges of trespass, criminal damage and theft. Fossil-collecting is, of course, not the same as the outlawed practice of egg-collecting. An egg may yet be a bird; leave a fossil and it may simply be lost for ever. Picking up a loose sample of something in abundant supply is unlikely to cause offence. However, in the case of a fossil which may be of value for its rarity, size or geological context, unauthorised removal is wholly out of order.

Laws exist to prevent damage or loss to much else besides fossils and minerals. Marine mammals are protected, as are most birds and all their eggs. Many plants too are on the protected species list (including sea-lavender and most orchids) and it is an offence to pick any such flowers. It is, in fact, illegal for anyone without permission of the owner to dig up any wild plant, including seaweed.

Additional layers of legal cover extend to those parts of the coastline which enjoy special status or protective ownership. The whole run from St Catherine's to Compton Chine is thus covered, as a Site of Special Scientific Interest, from which nothing may be removed without permission. Likewise National Trust territory, where bye-laws prohibit, among other things, the removal of plants, damage to trees, lighting of fires and leaving of litter. (Also forbidden, according to the notice at St Helens, are roller-skating and indecent language).

Seashore life is fragile. Visitors should respect the Country and Seashore Codes, taking care not to disturb or destroy what they come to enjoy. Tread cautiously, replace rocks the way you found them and, in the well-known lines:

Take nothing but pictures.
Waste nothing but time.
Leave nothing but footprints.

DOGS

Dog Prohibited and Permitted Beaches are a recent development, and current regulations may be summarised as follows:

South Wight Borough. Restrictions in force from 1st May to 30th September on council beaches in holiday areas (Sandown, Lake, Shanklin, Ventnor, Colwell) with clearly marked sections of beach in which no dog is allowed, apart from Guide Dogs. Except at Colwell, this leaves other marked sections of beach which are 'Dog Permitted/Clean-up Areas', where owners must clear up at once any mess made by dogs. Doggy-bins are provided and poop-scoops available from the Council, kiosks and pet-shops.

Medina Borough. Similar seasonal restrictions, creating dog-free zones along the top of the beaches at Ryde and Seaview. These extend only 100 metres out from the sea-wall, leaving a wide expanse of sand at low tide where dogs may run.

Other beaches. Outside Council control, such as Compton and Whitecliff Bay, have introduced their own summer dog-bans and further restrictions may follow.

NUDITY

Naturists have colonised Blackgang for a good many years. It's a long way to the shore, out of sight and off the beaten track enough to cause offence to no one. Nobody has to go there and nudity is not compulsory. In any case Continental practices have gradually crept in without fuss. Topless sunbathing is generally accepted and nudists have spread beyond Blackgang, though usually parked discreetly at the further end of the beaches. In all, a relaxed attitude prevails. There are no special bye-laws – the common law on decency covers all eventualities – and there are few reported instances of trouble. Sixty years have passed since beach-huts at Totland bore the warning, 'Bathing Dresses shall be to the reasonable satisfaction of the Bathing Attendants or Beach Inspector'.

JET-SKIS & MOTORBOATS

No doubt jet-skis will one day go the way of hula-hoops and the bubble-car. For the moment, though, they are extremely popular; also extremely unpopular. Jet-skis are undeniably noisy and they appear to threaten the safety of small children and swimmers in their vicinity, though many jet-skiers deny this. Existing bye-laws 'in respect of Seaside Pleasure Boats' (with fines up to £200) designate areas by main holiday-beaches where speed (not more than 10 knots), noise and safety restrictions are in force up to 200 metres out (300 in Sandown Bay). Meanwhile South Wight Borough Council, as part of its coastal management plan, is in the early stages of developing a strategy of beach-zoning. Arguments over jet-skis continue. . . .

FISHING

Apart from private beaches, harbours and piers, shore-fishing is generally un-restricted. Where there is public access to the foreshore, you are usually free to put out a rod and line, without licence or permit. Anglers and bathers have a common interest in keeping clear of each other and there is relatively little friction, thanks perhaps to the fact that the best fishing is to be had either at night or in winter or in spots generally unsafe or unsavoury to swim in. Yarmouth and Sandown Piers allow fishing (pay as you go), but Ryde Pier, with all its traffic, has had to limit fishing on grounds of safety to a small section for club-members with permits from Wightlink.

Further out, boat-trips are on offer through the season, operating mainly from Bembridge and Yarmouth. There are regular trips for deep-sea fishing and craft available for charter. For insurance and safety, always check that boat and owner are licensed, as well as sounding out local weather forecasts before putting out to sea.

USEFUL PHONE NUMBERS

Emergencies: 999 for services in real emergencies, incl. coastguard.
Police: 528000, routine enquires, 24 hours.
Coastguard: 95 552100, weather and general enquiries.
RSPCA: 93 231440.
St Mary's Hospital: 524081.
Isle of Wight County Council: 821000.
Medina Borough Council: 520000 (emergencies outside office hours – 821105).
South Wight Borough Council: 402175 (emergencies outside office hours – 821030).
Dog Wardens: 520000 (MBC) 852703 (South Wight).
National Trust: 526445.
IW Tourist Office: 524343. Tourist Information (Sandown) 403886.
S Vectis Bus Enquiries: 522456.
DIAL (Disablement Information Advice Line): 522823, the Riverside Centre, for information/enquiries on access, mobility, travel, local welfare services etc.
Water: Southern water 526611, 24 hours service.
National Rivers Authority – to report observed or suspected pollution, oil spillage, flooding etc., contact Winchester in office hours, 0962 713267. Also 24 hour emergency freefone, 0800 252676.
For general enquiries on water-quality, phone 822986 or Worthing, 0903 820692.

N.B. Almost all numbers given in the guide are I.O.W. numbers; they should be preceded by the area code (0983), if ringing from outside the Island.

TIDES

Every other week the tide comes right up at many points of the Island, making the difference between beach and no beach at all. A local tide-table is well worth its few pence. Tide times, but not heights, are also given on local radio coastal reports (around 07.30 and 17.30), blackboards in some resorts and in *The County Press*. Details in national papers (for Portsmouth, Dover or London Bridge) may be up to a couple of hours out for parts of the Island. Tidal computations are complex, nowhere more so than in the Solent area.

Tides alternate weekly between springs and neaps, following at a discreet distance the phases of the moon. Spring tides come up high and go out a long way; neaps have smaller variations. At new and full moons, sun and moon are in line with the Earth, pulling together to produce spring tides. At first and last quarters, sun and moon are at right angles to Earth, counteracting each other to give more modest neaps. Britain gets two high tides a day. With the moon belting round ahead of the Earth, high tide arrives 20 to 80 (on average 50) minutes later each day. The mathematics of this mean that the fortnightly spring tides always reach any one spot at about the same time of day – around midnight and noon on the I.O.W. (one hour sooner in W. Wight and one hour later BST). Six hours on from these times, the tide goes out furthest, leaving beaches most exposed. As a general guide, expect the tide to be up in the early afternoon of one weekend and down that time the following weekend.

Not moving in perfect circles, the moon and Earth reach positions at spring and autumn equinoxes (March, Sept.) when tides are most fully extended. Such events can be predicted far ahead; not so the weather. High pressure and N.E. winds will hold back local waters; a low barometer and S.W. gales will speed the tide's arrival and raise it one foot or more. January is commonly the time for such surges.

Curiously, the tide goes up and down almost twice as far at the eastern end of the Island than the west. Irregularities of the coastline combine with submarine contours to channel the sloshing of the sea into patterns of current and swirl that reach up to different levels along the coast. This partly explains why Bembridge lifeboat is parked at the end of a long runway off Foreland, while Yarmouth lifeboat can sit smug and ready at its harbour mooring.

Perhaps the most unusual feature of local waters is the double tide in the Western Solent. From Cowes to Freshwater, spring tides bring a second high-water 1-1½ hours after the first. At neaps there is a stand of about 2 hours. This gives boating folk in the creeks of Newtown and Yarmouth more time and extra water in which to potter. The bad news is that, with less time left to drain away, the ebb-tide runs with considerable force. No tide moves at the same rate throughout its 6 hours of ebb or flow. Slow to start and finish off, the tide has most speed in the middle 2 hours of its cycle.

WEATHER & SEA STATE

Isle of Wight weather is different – different even between Sandown and Shanklin, if you believe the sunshine and rainfall figures put out each day by the rival resorts. Most of the Island's weather comes in from the Atlantic – one earnest Victorian on the Undercliff noted in 40 years 8,584 winds from south and west, against 5,934 from north and east. The weather changes as it nears the coast, with winds affected up to ten miles out. At The Needles you can watch the clouds divide, most heading for the M27 into Hampshire, to the delight of sunbathers in Ryde.

Land and sea are rarely the same temperature and the difference between them (on average 5F) is the cause of fogs and breezes. The sea blankets the Island in winter, enabling Ventnor to claim frequent frost-free winters and seldom snow. By afternoon in spring and summer, hot air rises off the warmed land, pulling in cold sea-air to fill the gap. Onshore breezes explain why it's always stifling at home when you fancy a bathe and freezing by the time you get out of the car.

Sea-fogs arise through condensation when warm damp air passes over a cold surface – common along the coast in winter and spring. In summer and autumn, when the sea is coldest away from the shore, low banks of fog form out in the Channel and roll in on onshore winds. Such fogs last on average 6-10 hours, but can persist for 2-3 days.

Records show a curious tendency for 'good' summers on the Island to occur in odd calendar years, after a poor May – and vice versa. Over 65 years the last week in June has proved driest, November the wettest time of year and August often damp. June and July do best for sunshine, with Ryde clocking up a yearly average of 1750 hours of sunshine – 600 more than some towns in the industrial north. (All statistics by courtesy of Kenneth Hosking). The Island regularly tops the Sunshine League, without necessarily gaining the highest temperatures, thanks to the moderating influence of the sea.

Local radio stations give regular weather bulletins, while Radio 4 Shipping Forecast covers Wight (with Portland, Plymouth, Sole and Finisterre showing what is on its way). Telephone weather: HM Coastguard (95 552100), Soton Weather Centre (93 228844), Weathercall (0898 500 403).

Temperature. The sea round the Island is warm – warmer than round most of Britain anyway. The last recorded iceberg in this area was more than 60 years ago. Thanks to the Gulf Stream and a generous share of sunshine, Island waters reach their warmest, around 17C (65F), by August/September. The sea takes time to heat and is only ever really warm at the edge of shallow waters, as at Compton and Ryde. Equally slow to cool, the sea takes till Feb/March to drop to its minimum of around 7C (45F) or less at the edge, in places turning to mushy ice several times in recent years.

Conditions. The seas are getting rougher, with a doubling in frequency of large waves (above 16ft/5m) around our shores in the last 40 years. On average the Channel gets nasty (waves 10-35 ft, winds force 6-10) for 2-3 days a month in summer, 6-7 in winter. The more sheltered Solent is spared the worst of this.

CONCLUSION

Each year the Island loses seven acres to the sea. Some in sudden cliff collapses and some in the stealthy stripping of mudbanks and shoreline. At present Britain is growing slightly, with roughly one-third of the coastline static, one-third losing ground and a slightly larger third slowly building up. Wight's loss may be the Romney Marshes' gain.

Disastrous if it is your land or home that go over the cliff, but for some (like the Granville Fritillary butterfly) erosion creates homes and habitats of international importance. Erosion is an essential part of the dynamic process which is the coast. It is a feature to manage, not a problem to banish. Wholesale building of sea-walls is not the answer; wrapping the Island in a concrete corset would solve nothing. The best protector of land is the natural buffer of a well-nurtured beach.

The subject is given urgency by global warming, which threatens to raise sea-levels locally one to two feet by 2050, flooding parts of Cowes, Newport, Bembridge and, above all (or below all), Gurnard. The sea has always come in, and levels have risen nearly 10 feet since Roman times, but the present rate of increase (¼ inch per year) is something new.

Offshore dredging has long been blamed for vanishing beaches and dwindling fish-catches. Just under half a million tons of material is scooped out of the Solent and Spithead each year. Undoubtedly dredging can harm sites of marine archaeology (Bronze Age flint-axes appear not uncommonly in local cement-mixers), but the damage from gravel extraction may be nothing to compare with that done by inept coastal defences.

Beaches face other threats. Rows rumble on over development schemes intended to save the Island's economy, but more often destined for the Great Wight Elephant's Graveyard. The Island has a Victorian past worthy of conservation, but that heritage includes bold vision and confidence in the value of grand projects. Resorts must develop or else they decline.

The coastline is the Island's greatest asset. As such it needs to be cherished. Nothing shows better its present neglect than the rubbish that piles by the shore. Pollution, flooding and erosion are massive problems demanding political commitment and global resolve. But much can be done by individuals at ground-level. It needs only hands and eyes to tackle litter, safety and threats to nature. Increased supervision and regulation are not an unreasonable price to pay for our continuing enjoyment of the seashore. Perhaps the time has come for the Island to have beach-wardens seeing to each section of coast, on a year-round basis. Personally, after two years spent sampling every beach on the Island, I cannot imagine a more pleasant and worthwhile job.

ACKNOWLEDGEMENTS

The views and opinions expressed in this book are entirely my own, as are the errors.

In compiling this guide I approached a number of authorities and experts with a view to checking my facts. In every instance I met with extreme courtesy and kindness. I would like to record my sincerest thanks to the following for their considerable help and advice and for the trouble they took to explain things to me in terms I might understand:

Ken Harris, Leisure Services Officer, South Wight Borough Council; D. Jeffery, J. Slade, Environmental Services, SWBC; David King, Leisure and Tourism Office, Medina Borough Council; Tony Tutton, National Trust; Bob Edney, Countryside Management Service; Roger Herbert, Medina Valley Centre; Jonathan Cox, English Nature; Terry Smithson, Southen Water Services; Dave Lowthian, National Rivers Authority; John Trill, HM Coastguard; David Court, David Carter, SCOPAC; Steve Hutt, Geology Museum; Dr David Tomalin, David Motkin, IW Archaeological Unit; Clifford Webster, County Archivist; John Hilsum: Alan Parker; Doug Stephens, Angling Information Centre; Casualty Unit, Ryde Hospital; Wight Geogems; Kenneth Hosking: Mrs Corinne Brading, Gurnard; Rob Snow, Brighstone; Mark Coventry, marine biologist.

To the many anonymous Islanders who assisted with my inquiries, always in a friendly and welcoming manner, thanks indeed. I am indebted also to the friends (and, no doubt, ex-friends) who I pestered with questionnaires and inquiries, notably Linda Cobby, Cynara Crump, Rob and Sylvia Darby, the Feltons, Angela Forer, Tim Gurney, Pat Harwood, Howard Hawes, Ann and Les Jacobs, Tony Knight, Dee McCarty, Joan Matthew, Ken and Beryl Miller, Kieran and Margaret O'Donoghue, John Pearson, Joy Russell, Mr K. Strevens, Keith Terry, Barry Tomsett.

Finally, my thanks – and apologies – to Lindsey, my wife, and to David Burnett of the Dovecote Press, each of whom was frequently called upon to re-write sections of this book and to haul me out of the holes I dug myself into . . .

> They that go down to the sea in ships,
> that do business in great waters;
> These see the works of the Lord,
> and His wonders in the deep.

Psalm 107